HOME SERVICE
MILLIONAIRE

HOME SERVICE
MILLIONAIRE

How I Went from $50,000 in Debt to a $30 Million+ Business in Seven Years

TOMMY MELLO

Tommy Mello/Home Service Expert
2405 W. University Drive, Suite 102
Tempe, AZ 85281
homeserviceexpert.com
tommy@homeserviceexpert.com

Notice to Readers: Many links mentioned in this book are affiliate links. If you make a purchase through an affiliate link, my company will receive a commission on that sale.

Home Service Millionaire/Tommy Mello—1st ed.
ISBN: 9781732452107

THIS BOOK IS DEDICATED TO:

Tom Sr., Gina, Bill, and Kia,
for showing me what family is all about.

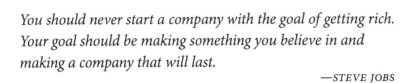

You should never start a company with the goal of getting rich. Your goal should be making something you believe in and making a company that will last.

—STEVE JOBS

CONTENTS

FOREWORD

Ara Mahdessian, CEO, ServiceTitan

Wherever you are in your home service business—Tommy Mello has been there. He has walked miles in your shoes. He has made the same mistakes, at multiple levels. He has stared down the many challenges of managing explosive business growth in a very short time to come out the other side—as a millionaire. And now he wants to help you do the same.

There are a million business books out there, so what makes this one different? The answer is Tommy. He is unique in that he isn't some guy who found success and then got out while he was ahead. He's still right there in the trenches every day, adapting and changing alongside the industry itself, and the information he offers in this book is indispensable if you're looking to grow profitably in today's challenging business climate.

Tommy is also the perfect person to learn from because he is still learning all the time, not just from books, but also directly from experts at the top of their game. As a result, he's a beast when it comes to modern marketing and growth methods. He has also seen firsthand how challenging it can be to grow solely through traditional marketing methods. That's why he has loaded this book with actionable advice on how to succeed with digital marketing. Tommy also really understands modern employment culture and how to make the workplace a desirable environment that high-performance team superstars will want to be a part of. You'll learn about that in this book too.

If you want to win, follow Tommy. He is a break-through-walls-to-make-it-happen kind of guy with huge ambitions and no fear. He sets crazy high goals and then finds a way to get them done, which often involves innovative ways to do things—many of which he shares in this book.

Best of all, he's giving it all back. We first met when he wrote me a bold pitch on why his company was a good fit for ServiceTitan and how he was going to make it work for the garage door service business. Then, working with us, he not only delivered on that promise, but also referred customers to us. Because of Tommy, ServiceTitan is now available to the entire garage door service industry, and we have a model for expanding into other industries.

If you implement a fraction of the strategies and tactics *Home Service Millionaire* offers, you will be better for it, in your business and in your life. And you'll be that much closer to what I know Tommy wants for all of you, which is to grow a profitable business into the millions so you can give back too. ▶▶▶

WHY THIS BOOK?

Home Service: A Million-Dollar Opportunity

If you're reading this book, chances are you already have a home service business but are just scraping by. Or you don't know how to grow because you can't possibly work anymore hours than you already are. (I sure know how *that* is.) This book aims to change all that in a big way.

Home service is a $400 billion-dollar industry with mammoth players such as Amazon, Google, and Bing. That's a four with *11 zeros* following. You know if the big boys are there, there is money to be made. You, too, can do very well as a local provider, and I'm going to tell you how.

The cool thing about home service is the need for it is never going away. Every home at some point requires maintenance. Over time, things break or wear out. Roofs need repairing, walls need painting, and drains need clearing. Your goal is to become the go-to company in your area for whatever home service you provide.

Why You Should Listen to Me

My primary company, A1 Garage Door Service, installs, repairs, and replaces garage doors. Today, I'm the primary owner of 14 companies, with more than 250 employees in 12 states. We produced more than $30 million in revenue last year, and this year we're on track to cross the $40 million mark with plans to expand even more.

I've invested hundreds of thousands of dollars and spent hundreds of hours with mentors and experts all over the country who have shared their knowledge and systems with me, so I know firsthand how life changing having the right people pointing you in the right direction can be. I'll be sharing the most important things I've learned in this book. There's also a list of books by the key mentors and experts who have influenced me at the end of this book, as well as even more resources at homeservicemillionaire.com/resources.

My Story

I wasn't born with a silver spoon in my mouth. In Sterling Heights, Michigan, where I grew up, I learned young that if I wanted something, I had to go out and get it. Nothing was about to fall into my lap.

My first hustle, before I was out of high school, was shoveling snow and mowing lawns. By my mid-20s, I'd built that into a successful full-time landscaping business.

Next, thanks to my mentor, Dave Carson, I expanded my landscaping business and started installing drip irrigation systems for large companies.

While I was making what I thought was great money with that business (as well as a bartending job), one of my roommates, Sean, got a job answering the phone at a garage door repair company for $40,000 a year. Sean then got my other roommate, Gabe, a job as a garage door technician. And Gabe was making even *more* money—$70,000 a year.

Naturally, the entrepreneur in me was curious. I said to Gabe, "What can go wrong with a garage door? And how the hell are you making that kind of cheese?!"

Gabe said, "Tommy, you've got to check out the garage door business. It's badass!" And so I closed my drip-system company and became a garage door tech too. I continued bartending and flipping cars, though. Having a bunch of different income streams is just who I am. (Ask me about my Christmas light business.)

Anyway, Gabe is an amazing salesman. He understood that if we fixed the problem on our first visit, word would spread and we'd get new customers. We created a sales funnel based on that premise and sales went through the roof!

Seeing the potential, I decided to go into partnership with Gabe in the garage door business. I thought, "I'm a master at marketing and Gabe's an amazing salesman. What could possibly go wrong?" We started advertising in several mailers and ran Yellowbook ads. Soon, we were making bank!

Then, the economy tanked. It was the worst recession anyone I knew in Arizona had ever seen. I mean it was *bad*. It hit our business *hard*.

The thing is, there was no *lack* of business. In fact, we were absolutely slammed. We were taking calls, running jobs, fixing trucks, controlling inventory, dealing with upset customers, doing taxes, emptying wastebaskets, and everything else.

Family? Friends? Date night? Vacations? Weekends? Not happening.

A year later, we were still struggling to pay the bills. We owed everyone and their brother, and before we knew it the business was $50,000 in debt. We needed to turn things around—and fast.

I offered to take on all the debt myself if Gabe would dissolve the partnership and I could become the sole owner. Gabe agreed on the spot and within a few months we'd figured it out, with a minimum of stress.

It was now only me, with $50,000 in debt and no employees. That was the bad news. The good news, at least the way I saw it, was whether this company was going to make it or not was now 100 percent on me. And so I got to work.

First, it was crazy to me that we could be so busy and still be losing money. I was determined to figure that out.

The problem was, since Gabe was gone, I was now a one-man show. I worked 10- to 12-hour days on average. There were longer days that didn't end until midnight. I was owner, technician, and office manager all in one. I was perpetually exhausted and constantly worried, but I refused to fail.

In the truck between jobs, I read books on business and entrepreneurship. I went for my MBA, squeezing in classes and studying until midnight so I could expand my knowledge and apply what I'd learned to my business.

As if that wasn't tough enough, my girlfriend at the time left me. She felt she had taken a back seat to my business—and she was right. There wasn't much time left over for anything—or anyone—else at that point. It was do or die.

I doubled down on my millionaire mindset, got some checks and balances in place, and cranked up the growth and lead-generation machines. Within a few months, I started to gain momentum and cash flow began to loosen up. I hired my first employee, then my second, and then my third. And the customers kept on coming.

Seven years later, the Mello Home Service empire is making more than $30 million a year and has more than 250 employees in 12 states.

The rest, as they say, is history.

What I want you to take away from this story is if I can turn my business around and grow it into the millions, so can you—*if* you're willing to change how you think about achieving your goal and you're willing to work on yourself.

If you can open your mind and commit to consistently improving yourself, the information I'm going to share with you may change your life. I know it did mine. If you're up for the challenge, you too can become a home service millionaire.

Ethics and Honesty

I'm going to be up front with you. Being ethical and honest is important to me—more important than making money—and I think making money is pretty important!

So if you're coming with me, I'm going to insist that you do all of this in an honest and ethical way and that you hold anyone who associates with you—managers, employees, vendors, and others—to the same standards.

I believe in treating employees right and giving customers the best-quality product and service possible, even if it means I make a little less financial profit in the end. It's more important to me that I can look in the mirror at night and feel good about myself and what I'm creating for both my employees and my customers.

You'll notice this value of mine—ethics and honesty—reappearing throughout this book. Why? Because it's easy to make a case for cutting corners and looking the other way. It's called "creative justification." It happens all the time. And I guarantee you're going to be tempted, especially when you're struggling.

Don't do it. You can be ethical and honest and still build a great business. In fact, ethics and honesty are at the foundation of my success.

You with me?

Good. Here's how it's all going to work.

How This Book Works

In a nutshell, you're going to learn my proven framework for building a successful home service business, and I'm going to provide you with tons of resources you can use to propel yourself toward your goal. In the first chapter, you'll learn how to think like a millionaire when it comes to focus, attitude, and priorities. I'll ask you to consider why you want to be in business in the first place and explain why having a strong "why" to rely on is vital—especially when things get tough (and they will get tough). I want you to be able to withstand the discomfort and stress that is an unavoidable part of building a multi-million-dollar business.

In the second chapter, you'll learn the key operating systems I use to run my businesses, starting with organizational charts, which allow your team to understand what their responsibilities are and exactly what's expected of them, and operating manuals, which are documented processes that tell your staff exactly how you want them to do 80 percent of their job. I'll explain why an integrated customer relationship management (CRM) system (e.g., ServiceTitan) is at the heart of every successful home service business. It puts a lot of tools at your techs' fingertips, allowing them to better serve the customer and make more sales. It also allows you to have real-time access to the data you need to be able to track how your business is doing by monitoring key performance indicators (KPIs). I'll discuss the eight KPIs you should focus on first to get a handle on how your business is doing. I'll address what you need to think about to determine and then optimize the marketing spend required to get to the revenue number you're after. I'll explain the three elements of business success: people, processes, and technology. Finally, I'll point out five key things you'll need to fix before you can step on the gas.

In chapter three, I'll reveal how you can turn your business into a growth machine with marketing. Marketing is my passion. It's also a major key to my success, so I'm not going to hold anything back. I'll start slow, sharing some tactics you can implement right away that will help your business, and then I'm going to ramp it up from there. I'll cover branding, building your online reputation, dominating search, customer referral programs, traditional marketing methods, and business partnerships. You might get a little overwhelmed by the end, but don't worry. Absorb as much as you can and write down all your questions. I won't leave you hanging—I've got a team ready and waiting to help you out.

With some marketing tactics in play, I'll discuss lead-generation strategies in chapter four, and then, in chapter five, I'll explain the eight-step sales process I teach my technicians, how to overcome customer objections, and more. I'll also address how to take care of those customers after the service call so they'll buy from you again and refer you to their friends. It gets a little deep by the end, but hang in there. You'll be better for it.

In chapter six, I'll explain how you can become a performance powerhouse. Apple computers icon Steve Jobs once said, "A small team of A+ players can run circles around a giant team of B and C players." I'll outline exactly what you need to do to find and recruit those A+ players and share my secrets on how to effectively train and manage them so they can help drive your company forward faster.

Finally, in chapter seven, I'll wrap up all of this advice nice and neat and tell you about what's next. Throughout the book, I'll be sharing personal stories as well as insights from my mentors and even a few of my heroes. I want to bring this information to life so you can absorb as much as possible and be on your way to creating your seven-figure home service business right away.

I can't promise you will have a multimillion-dollar business overnight, but if you're willing to work hard, open your mind, and stay true to yourself, you can make it big, not just in the home service business but in *any* business you choose.

Ready? Let's get started. ▶▶▶

CHAPTER 1

THE MILLIONAIRE MINDSET

Since you're reading a book called *Home Service Millionaire*, I am assuming your goal is to become rich but you're not sure how to get there. For starters, I suggest you focus on becoming *wealthy* instead.

Rich vs. Wealthy

The word *rich* means you have loads of money in the bank, but no recurring income. *Wealthy*, on the other hand, means you have a steady flow of income feeding your bank account each week, even if you're on vacation. A business run correctly can give you more wealth than you ever dreamed of.

In *The Millionaire Next Door*, authors Thomas J. Stanley and William D. Danko found that people who become wealthy allocate their time, energy, and money in ways consistent with enhancing their net worth. They also found that although the unwealthy spend more time *worrying* about their financial situations than the wealthy do, they spend very little time actually *doing* anything about it.

Ouch. If that's you, it's OK. You can change. This book will help.

To sustain yourself as you build wealth, you'll need a reason for your business to exist that goes beyond making money. You need to find your "why."

Let me explain.

If you're like most home service business owners, you probably worked as a technician for someone else and you weren't happy. One day you woke up and thought, "Forget this guy. I can make more money working for myself." Your "why" at that point was to stop working for someone else and make more money. You probably didn't understand all that was going to be involved with being on your own. All you knew was you had to go.

Things were probably OK at first, but as the bills piled up and you went through your first dip you realized there was more to running a successful home service business than you originally thought. You started thinking you should have just changed jobs rather than gone out on your own.

And that's exactly why not wanting to work for someone else is not a strong enough "why" to sustain yourself as you do what you need to do to build a multimillion-dollar home service business.

What you need to do now is focus on why you want to have a business in the first place—why it really exists—because you're going to need to tap into that "why" to keep going when things get tough.

"For the past 33 years, I have looked in the mirror every morning and asked myself: 'If today were the last day of my life, would I want to do what I am about to do today?' And whenever the answer has been 'No' for too many days in a row, I know I need to change something."

—STEVE JOBS

Finding Your "Why"

In 2009, author, speaker, and marketing consultant Simon Sinek gave a TEDx talk called "How Great Leaders Inspire Action." It was so popular he was invited to take it to the main TED stage. The video of that talk has 7.8 million views as of this writing. (Check it out. It's on YouTube.) At the core of Simon's presentation was this idea: people don't buy *what* you do, they buy *why* you do it. He said any organization can explain *what* it does, some can explain *how* they do it, but very few can clearly articulate *why*. Why is not money or profit—those are results. Simon challenges you to ask why—why your company exists, why your customers should buy from you, and why your employees should stay.

So take a minute and think about it: Why does your home service business exist? (Beyond "not wanting to work for someone else" or "making money.")

I'll use a couple of my businesses as an example. The Home Service Expert network exists to improve the lives of hundreds of thousands of entrepreneurs by helping them start their own businesses on a strong foundation, while sharing with other business owners the key ingredients to boost their growth.

Here's another one: A1 Garage Door Service exists to make customers feel safe. A good-quality, well-maintained garage door makes customers feel safe because they know the largest entrance to their home is not only attractive, but also solid, secure, and will work flaw-lessly for years to come.

The reason not wanting to work for someone else is not a good "why" is because it's too easy to bail out when things go south. It's only ever about you. To keep going when things get interesting, you need a "why" that goes beyond not wanting to work for someone else or making money to improving the lives of others.

A "why" like this will also allow you to inspire your employees so they will come to love what they do as much as you do and natu-rally communicate that passion to your customers. That enthusiasm and belief in the importance of what they are doing will automatically differentiate you from your competitors—big-time.

How will your home service business improve the lives of others? What legacy will you leave? What is your "why"?

Zeroing in on Your "Why"

Think about how you could run your business so it and your "why" are aligned. A good place to start is thinking about what you want people to say at your funeral. I'm serious. What do you want your life and your business to have meant to others when it's all over with? Write that down on a piece of paper.

Think about what good things you could accomplish through your business that no one else could. Write that down too.

Now, look at what you wrote. What do those things tell you about what's most important to you?

If you can't seem to find a compelling "why" for having a home service business beyond not wanting to work for anyone else or making money, or you really hate everything about having a business except the actual work—meaning financials, marketing, sales, and managing others—and you aren't willing to learn and grow into it, you might want to rethink your plan. Those things are not going away. In fact, if you do this right, you'll be out of the field sooner rather than later and those things will be the bulk of what you are focusing on day to day.

Very successful people have a purpose that goes beyond their own personal benefit. They're excited, dedicated, passionate, and fearless in pursuit of that purpose, and that energy inspires everyone around them. The energy they radiate is what people respond to first, before anything they say. That energy comes directly from their "why." It's what gives them the guts to keep going when things get tough.

Do You Own a Business or a Job?

Robert Kiyosaki, author of *Rich Dad Poor Dad*, said, "A business is ownership and control of a system and the ability to lead people." If you have a *business*, you can step away for a week or two, and between the system and your people who are trained on it, everyone knows what to do and the business can keep going without you.

But if the business goes away whenever you do, you own a *job*. What if you have employees but no systems that allow you to step away from working *in* the business so you can work *on* it? You still own a job—a big one that has probably turned out to be a lot more stressful than your original job working for someone else.

The first step in converting a job into a business is implementing business systems. I'll talk more about that topic in the next chapter.

The Business You're Always Becoming

Life and business strategist Tony Robbins once said, "Anticipation is power. In today's fractured and evolving business landscape, owners and leaders need to run two businesses simultaneously—the one you're in now and the one you're always becoming."

If you decide to commit to a vision of having a well-run business, you are automatically in two businesses: the messed-up one you have now with no "why," no systems and processes in place, and no accountability, and the better-run business you are working on becoming.

I'll warn you now—being in two businesses like this is hard. You'll need to make some tough choices. You'll probably feel some short-term pain. That's OK. You'll live through it. And you will *love* the result.

You Are in Business to Make a Profit

I've heard a lot of business owners complain that there's no way they can charge more than $300 for a repair. The problem with this approach is since they aren't making enough money to cover what things should cost, they short themselves on their paycheck and pay their people just above minimum wage with no benefits—and then wonder why they have so much turnover!

How do 99.9 percent of business owners come up with pricing? They go along with market trends without taking time to figure out what it really costs to run a service call, much less run the office or determine how much money they want to land in their wallet at the end of the day.

A1 Garage is not the cheapest option available because what our customers are looking for is a garage door service with a great customer experience and technicians who are skilled, dependable, and safe. This means well-trained technicians who have been background checked and drug tested; new trucks that do not break down and are efficient on gas; better warranties; and the best technology in the industry, such as Uber-like tracking that texts customers when the technician is on the way.

Does this cost money? Hell yes, it does! But A1 Garage is getting more than 7,000 opportunities a month, so we must be doing something right.

If you don't have enough money to put these things in place, you're probably not charging enough. Not charging enough severely limits your growth potential. It forces you, the owner, to either do all the jobs yourself or assign them to a technician who is so overloaded he's always running late. If you don't charge enough, you may also find you're still out in the field at age 65 because you can't afford to retire. You don't have time or energy to work *on* the business because you're always working *in* it.

See if any of these descriptions apply to you:

1. You don't understand that after you pay all the bills, your employees, and yourself, there should still be a large amount of money left over—i.e., profit.
2. You can't charge $300 for a repair because your ticket price is so low and you don't have any top performers who can not only make service calls but also sell stuff.
3. You think you own a business, but you really own a big, unruly, and unrewarding job.

You're in business to make a profit. And to make sure you are operating in a way that will create the profit you want to make, you need to know how your business is doing at all times. Speaking of profit, you'll want to make sure the financial end of your business is set up in a way that you can not only maximize it but also hang onto it. Surround yourself with financial professionals you trust who understand your industry and keep you apprised of what your financial position is at all times.

Ellen Rohr is a serial entrepreneur (currently president of Zoom Drain, a drain and sewer franchise) and a small-business financial expert who has worked with tons of home service business owners. Ellen views business as a game; here's how you can play to win. ▶▶▶

HOW TO PLAY AND WIN THE BUSINESS GAME

Ellen Rohr, Business Un-Complicated

The game of business is easy once you learn the rules. If I can learn them, so can you. I made tons of mistakes in our family business for years until I finally learned the rules from some great mentors.

It was plumbing business legend Frank Blau Jr. who taught me the most important rule, which is to charge more than it costs to be in business. Why? Because when do that you create a profit—money you make from sales above and beyond what you need to pay your bills. Who doesn't want more of that? (Or at least some of that!)

When you take that profit in cash (as opposed to letting it decompose in accounts receivable), you can use it to grow your business—or turn around a bad financial situation. Money buys options. Money can fix things. Not everything, but just about everything is easier with some cash on hand.

Another one of my mentors is Warren Buffet. I have never met him, but he taught me, through his book, that in business there is ultimately one financial scorecard: the balance sheet. And every other financial report is a subset of the balance sheet. Here's what you need to know.

The balance sheet is based on the following equation: assets = liabilities + equity. This equation is in line with the universal law—what goes around comes around. Or, for every action there is a reaction. It's how we keep financial score in the business game. So we're on the same page, let's define the terms:

1. Assets: The "stuff" the company owns. Anything of value—cash, accounts receivable, trucks, inventory, or land—is an asset.

2. Liabilities: These are sources of assets, how you got the "stuff." These are claims against assets by someone other than you (the owner). This is a reflection of what your company *owes*. Notes payable, taxes payable, and loans are liabilities.

3. Equity: Equity includes funds that have been supplied to the company to get the "stuff." Equity also reflects ownership of the assets earned through profitability. Equity shows ownership of the assets or claims against the assets, a reflection of what the company *owns*.

Warren Buffet wins big in the game of business again and again by buying and building companies that make profits. Here are his two rules for business:

1. Protect the assets: The assets are your "stuff"—what you have. The first financial objective is to protect the wealth you have.

2. Grow the assets: The second financial objective is to expand the "stuff." Grow cash and other assets.

That's the game! Let's look at the three ways you can grow assets:

1. Through Liabilities: You can borrow money. When you buy a new truck, and get a loan for that truck, assets go up and the liability (a loan) goes up. (Maybe you have already overdone this. It's easy to get too deep in debt.)

2. Through Owner Investment: You can put your own money into the company. Perhaps when you got started you wrote a check from your personal account and opened up your business account. Assets go up and the owner's investment (an equity account) goes up. Are you looking for venture capital? If an investor cuts a check and puts it in your checking account, then his owner's equity goes up. At that point, he may own more of your company than you do. Just be aware.

3. Through Profits: Sell stuff for more than it costs and create profits. Assets go up and net income goes up. This year's profits show up in the equity section of your balance sheet. When you lose money—sell stuff for less than it costs you—equity goes down and assets go down. That's the elegant, beautiful, sometimes horrible truth of the balance sheet. Another benefit of profit is you can use it to pay down your debt! Instead of always trying to get by on less, consider how you can make more profit.

Are you winning or losing the game? Let's find out. First, make sure your balance sheet is right. Don't make decisions on messy or erroneous information. Clean up the accounts and get them current. Then, take a look at the numbers.

If you have more liabilities than assets, you are going backward. You'll have a negative equity balance. The long-term fix is to address the reason you got in trouble in the first place. For one, you have to charge more than it costs. And you have to have enough sales at the right price to cover all expenses and make a profit. You might be able to borrow more money, and you might be tempted to put more of your own money into the company. You might even entice an investor to infuse some cash. However, the only way to create wealth is to generate profits.

The first step to fixing this problem is to create a budget. Frank Blau Jr. suggests that you start a budget by listing all your expenses. Jot down—in a spreadsheet or on a columnar pad—what you want to spend on you and your team. Put in proper salaries and wages for the wonderful, skilled, valuable work you do. Then, address every expense account and be generous. Provide nice trucks, uniforms, benefits, and marketing dollars. Hold your chin up as you create a budget based on reasonable expenses to do what you do really well.

Then, put in the amount of sales you want. Make the sales total bigger than the expenses and add your desired amount of profit to that number. Then, take that sales amount and divide it up by the number of "widgets" you could sell. If you sell labor, your widget is an hour or a day—a unit of time. If you sell products, divide the sales up by the number of products you could sell. Sometimes it's a combo platter. Play out a few scenarios.

When you do this, as I did, you will discover that your selling price is higher than a lot of your competitors. Gulp.

Frank knew this would be the case. He had seen it hundreds of times before. His advice: be better, faster, stronger, nicer, more current, better equipped—or all of those things. Be a better marketer and salesperson so you can communicate why and how you are better. So when I balked at raising my prices, he said, "Charging what it costs to do a great job is in the customer's best interest." Isn't that a head flip? It sure was for me. But think about it: when you play this way, customers will get better service and be happier, and you will make the profits you need and deserve to make for working so incredibly hard. And that means everybody wins.

For more information about how to win the business game financially, visit homeservicemillionaire.com/financial.

CHAPTER 2

CHECKS AND BALANCES MACHINE

How crazy it is that McDonald's, a multibillion-dollar global corporation, can be run on a foundation of teenagers who possess a bare minimum of work skills? The key to its success is business systems.

McDonald's has operating manuals that cover everything required to run the business—from restaurant design to hiring to product delivery to the finer details of customer interaction. For example, did you know there is a wash station in the kitchen where employees key in their employee code every time they wash their hands? McDonald's has software that runs reports on all of these things.

Can you imagine hiring people with no work experience and turning them loose in your business without training them to do the job or explaining your standards? Without documented business systems and training, even your people who do have work experience are probably not doing things the way you want. You're still putting out the same fires week after week, and your business is either out of control or stuck in neutral.

The bad news is it's going to stay that way until you put certain systems into place that will allow you to grow and scale.

For starters, everyone in the business needs to have a clear understanding of their responsibilities and the results you expect. And everyone needs be held accountable to actually do what your systems and processes dictate.

To achieve this goal, there needs to be a set of checks and balances that allows you to determine how effective your systems and processes are so you can determine who or what is working, not working, or just plain missing.

Holding employees accountable to systems and processes is challenging enough, but holding yourself accountable to stop and do what's needed to grow the business is even harder! That's why we suggest you retain a business coach who can advocate for your goals, greatly increasing the chances you'll spend time working *on* the business instead of *in* it.

Think of it like a personal trainer for your business. A personal trainer helps with diets, supplements, workout plans, and times to eat, sleep, and do cardio so you can get the body you want. A business coach holds you accountable to do the things you need to do to get the business you want. (Hint: We can help. Go to homeserviceexpert.com /discovery-call/ and schedule a call.)

Organizational Charts

One check and balance is a clear and flat organizational chart. An organizational chart allows you to communicate clearly what people's roles are based on their titles, what results you expect from them, and, more importantly, how they can move up in your company.

Visualize the ultimate company and figure out every role you need to run it, even if there's no person filling that role yet. Important: Don't create or adjust the roles based on the existing personalities in your company. Always organize around roles. Once you've determined the roles required to run your company, fill them based on someone's skill set and training. Don't change the box to fit the person. (Go to homeservicemillionaire.com/org-chart to see a great picture of A1 Garage Door Service's monster organizational chart.)

Operating Manuals

Another set of checks and balances is operating manuals. Operating manuals are a collection of objective and clearly written policies and procedures that have been proven to deliver the results you want. If you want people to do things the same way, you need to write down the way you want it done, make an operating manual, train people using that manual, and then hold them accountable to doing it your way.

I know what you might be thinking. "Manual? We have an office manual and no one ever opens it!" These manuals are different. They should lay out 80 to 90 percent of what each role in the company does 80 percent of the time. Employees live, sleep, and breathe these manuals because they clearly outline what you expect. Once everyone is trained on them, operating manuals allow you to do five things:

1. Ensure everyone is doing things the same way—your way—whether someone has been with the company a few months or a few years.
2. Instill accountability into your company culture.
3. Replicate your business across town or in another city.
4. Prevent fires rather than running around putting out the same ones you put out yesterday.
5. Stop waiting around for the only employee who knows how to do a certain task because anyone can be trained using the manual.

Al Levi, The 7-Power Contractor, is the master of operating manuals. I hired him to get ours in place. He's not doing a lot of one-on-one consulting anymore, so I was lucky he agreed to do it. It has already made a huge difference in my company. I really thought we were OK until Al walked through my shop and pointed out all the opportunities we were missing by not having an organizational chart in place and operating manuals that tell my techs, customer service representatives (CSRs), and dispatchers how I want them to do their jobs. Al is a fountain of information on running a contracting business, and he has agreed to share even more of his wisdom with you in the next section.

SYSTEMATIZING YOUR HOME SERVICE BUSINESS
Al Levi, The 7-Power Contractor

There aren't a million things to learn in a home service business . . . there are seven. The first one is planning power. What I know is this: if you don't have a plan you are planned for. I worked for 25 years in every aspect of my family's plumbing, heating, cooling, and electrical business, and we got planned for all the time—for years! We were putting out fires one day only to have them restart the next. It was exhausting. The good thing was we were making money, but I knew if something didn't change my brothers and I would be a bunch of rich dead guys.

One stressful day, I was looking for someone to help me with a critical project. I went from desk to desk asking, but no one had time. I blew a gasket. I said, "Grab whatever you are working on and meet me in the conference room." My employees piled their papers in the middle of the conference table and I started to go through them. I discovered two people who were working on the same project and didn't know it. I also found several projects whose owners swore were of top importance to me that I didn't even know were out there!

To fix this problem, we inventoried all of the projects and put them on a master project list. This list is the catchall for every project or new habit you think you want to work on (or are working on) in your company. Most master project lists have about 100 to 150 projects on them. The next step was to funnel those projects down to a top 30 list of projects or habits we would focus on in the coming year.

The problem is we couldn't work on 30 things at the same time or none would get the attention they needed. We only have three things in this life—time, energy, and money—and they only go so far. So once we had our top 30 list, we applied the criteria that the project or habit needed to solve our biggest problem or challenge, or give us the greatest chance to grow and be profitable. Then we got the list down to just five things, which we called our top five list.

I then devoted a portion of my week to working on those projects. As soon as I finished one, I promoted another to the top five list from the top 30.

The top five list is really about working on the right thing, at the right time, in the right way—and it works.

The one thing that always lands on a new client's top five list is systematizing the business. What I mean by that is, if I gave you five great plumbers and you sent them to five different jobs to set a toilet, would they all do it the same way? The answer is no. If you sent five great electricians, garage techs, or roofers out to five jobs, would they all do things the same way? No.

That's why you have to get those procedures out of your head and in writing so people don't have to read your mind. There should be a manual for every box on your organizational chart, meaning the boxes it takes to run your company. That manual should describe 80 percent of what you do. You'll never cover 100 percent. If you get the 80 percent of routine things you do all the time written down, the remaining 20 percent won't throw you for a loop.

In my manuals, there is nothing longer than a page because it's not like you've never done your trade before. You're already trained; I'm just trying to get you to do it the way I want you to do it. The same thing goes for your CSRs, dispatchers, and technicians, as well as your accounts payable and accounts receivable people—everyone that has a box on the organizational chart should have a corresponding manual to follow.

To systematize your business, you must document the policies and procedures in an objective way, which is the only way to run your company if you're looking for less stress and more success.

There are five additional powers—financial power, staffing power, selling power, marketing power, and sales coaching power—but planning and operating power are the two that will change your business for the better the fastest, so that is where you should start.

If you're in the plumbing, heating, cooling, or electrical business, visit homeservicemillionaire.com/operating-manuals to find out more about how operating manuals can change your business for the better.

Use Checklists

At A1 Garage, we have checklists for everything. To make this job easier, I'm developing a checklist program called Checklist Assist, which will allow you to create custom checklists on the fly, complete with the ability to include videos, photos, and more. For more information on Checklist Assist, visit homeservicemillionaire.com /checklist.

Invest the time and money in creating organizational charts, operating manuals, and checklists. They'll change your business for the better—I know they have changed mine.

There's a great story in *The E-Myth Revisited* by Michael Gerber about a hotel he visited that always provided flawless and very personalized service. When he inquired how the hotel was able to do this, the manager explained that it was the result of its operating manuals and comprehensive checklists. This system led staff members to ask guests a series of questions, which allowed them to record and then meet individual preferences. Your operating manuals and checklists are the key to providing consistently outstanding customer service that will allow your business to grow.

Delegate Authority

When you were launching your home service business, you did everything yourself: installations and repairs, getting the oil changed in the truck, answering phones, balancing the books, and talking to the loan officers. You even cleaned the bathroom in the shop. Maybe you still do!

But if you want to grow your business, you'll need to learn to delegate as many of those routine tasks as soon as possible. For some people, this can be tough—especially if you're used to being seen as a superhero. You want to control everything, because you feel you're the only one who can do the job correctly. You're so busy trying to save a few pennies, you're missing the hundred-dollar bills flying over your head. Here's a question: If the people working for you are so incompetent that you can't hand off even the most routine or repetitive task to them, why are they still working for you?

Or maybe you're the type who can't say "no" when you need to. To avoid conflict, you take on work others should really be doing.

The problem with both of these scenarios is that you'll eventually become overwhelmed and, as a result, you'll start making bad decisions. (There are only so many hours in a day.) And that's no good for anyone. Here are seven steps you can take to begin delegating some of those repetitive tasks:

1. Select the routine or repetitive task you want to delegate.
2. Create a procedure that outlines the correct way to perform the task, step by step. Be sure to document the who, what, where, when, why, and how of the task.
3. Set deadlines and then hold people to them. I believe in Parkinson's Law, which is, "Work expands to fill the time available."
4. Document the expected results of the delegated task.
5. Assign the task to someone, and then, using the procedure, train him or her on how to do it. Make sure the person signs off and accepts responsibility for the task.
6. Let them perform! Don't micromanage, but make sure you are kept in the loop on progress and performance. Give constant feedback and recognition along the way. (This is key for all humans—we need to know how we are doing.) Make a note on your calendar to follow up a few days before the task is due to see how it's going.
7. Evaluate the results and revise the procedure if necessary.

Over time, you'll want to collect these procedures and publish them as your company's operating manual.

One of the biggest traps for small companies is when you're doing a lot of work that doesn't align with your primary role as leader. Hire the best people in their specialties (accounting, marketing, legal, etc.) and then *supervise* them—don't do the work for them.

Caution: It is possible to go too far with delegation. An absentee owner—the guy who delegates everything—is just as bad as the guy who does it all or micromanages.

Your most important job as a leader is to foster a positive company culture and model its values, resolve conflicts, oversee hiring, mentor the senior management team, and monitor financing and budgets. Delegate everything else!

CRM: He Who Has the Best Data Wins

See if this sounds familiar: customer data is spread out over office productivity suite documents, mobile phone data, email systems, and maybe even Rolodex entries or paper note cards. Key information and messages get misplaced or overlooked. That's what it was like in our office before we implemented an integrated customer relationship management (CRM) system, in our case, ServiceTitan.

Don't get me wrong; there are a ton of decent CRM systems out there. The problem is unless your scheduling, dispatch, service, sales, marketing, inventory, payroll, agreements, and accounting are all under one roof, your staff will have to check and input things into multiple systems, and I'll tell you something right now—it will never happen. Without all this stuff under one roof, you can't get good data, and without good data you can't make accurate decisions about how to improve and ultimately grow your home service business. Here are just a few things ServiceTitan allowed us to do:

1. Help technicians improve close rates, increase sales, and increase the revenue they get on those sales.
2. Automate a lot of back-office, manual tasks so it takes fewer people to manage the business.
3. Deliver a better customer experience. We can now text the customer with a picture and description of the tech, and the customer can track his estimated time of arrival similar to how Uber works. We can also email customers to offer deals and wish them a happy birthday. And the system prompts us to reach out to those customers with service agreements to schedule a time for their annual appointment.
4. Track which ads are working by assigning a unique phone number to each campaign—Valpak, Yelp, newspaper, etc.—which is tagged to the customer and follows the job around so we know how much revenue each ad generates, and we can do more of it and less of what's not performing.

The list goes on. Without an integrated CRM system—correction, without ServiceTitan—we would never be in the growth mode we are in today.

At this time, ServiceTitan is only available to plumbing, heating, cooling, electrical, and garage door businesses. It is the best CRM system for those businesses, but there are other options. If you need to grow a little more before you bring on ServiceTitan, you can check out something like Housecall Pro. Housecall Pro is a little more manual, but anything is better than chasing paper all over the office. The sooner you can bring on ServiceTitan the better. (For more information about Housecall Pro, go to homeservicemillionaire.com/housecall.)

The other major reason you need a CRM in place is that you need to be able to see and monitor certain sets of numbers to make sure your business stays on track. You may think you know what the numbers are, but unless you have a CRM system in place to capture and crunch that data, I can pretty much guarantee—you don't. And if you don't have good numbers, you can't run your business with key performance indicators.

To provide you with more insight about why having a CRM system in place is so important, I asked Ara Mahdessian, chief executive officer of ServiceTitan, to discuss what you need to know to grow your business in today's changing customer landscape.

GROWING YOUR HOME SERVICE BUSINESS WITH CRM

Ara Mahdessian, CEO, ServiceTitan

Adapting to Consumers' Changing Expectations

The greatest challenge and opportunity home service businesses face is changing consumer expectations and how consumers are interacting with businesses today.

Every other industry has either adapted or died. Look at what happened to the taxi industry with Uber. The taxi industry didn't adapt, so Uber came in and crushed it. The same thing happened in the restaurant industry with OpenTable, and now it is happening in home service too.

Consumers want to do business with home service businesses differently. They want to be able to do things like text your company and get a response, as well as book an appointment or follow up on an existing appointment.

They also want to know things like who is going to be showing up at their house when they're home alone, and exactly when that technician is going to arrive so they're not sitting around waiting and getting pissed off. When a customer is angry before the job even starts, the tech isn't going to get that sale, no matter what they propose.

Those home service businesses that adapt quickly and well to these new expectations are going to thrive. The businesses I see growing by leaps and bounds and making millions more dollars and increasing profits are the ones that are giving customers what they want and doing a great job at it. These businesses provide amazing customer service on the phone. They text their customers and interact with them online. They send the customer the tech's profile before he arrives so they know who to expect, and they allow the customer to track the tech's whereabouts and estimated time of arrival through text or email.

Once at the customer's home, the tech presents the options beautifully on an iPad, complete with finance options that are automatically calculated—no more chicken scratches on the invoice.

Then, when the job is done, the customer gets a review request, so they know the company takes their satisfaction seriously. Afterward, the company reads the review and immediately takes action on the feedback.

Finding Great Talent and Training Them Constantly

The number one obstacle, especially for growing companies (other than having the necessary systems in place), is having great people in place. And today it's incredibly hard to find the right talent, especially in the field.

The face of your company is that tech in the customer's home. Home is the most intimate place for your customer. How do you find people who not only know the trade but also are really good at communicating with customers? It's hard enough to find a great tech; it's almost impossible to find someone who is both a great tech *and* a great communicator. So how do you solve this problem?

One is with a big investment in training, and I think A1 Garage does a great job of that. The other thing is enabling people to succeed by providing them with the tools that allow them to become really good at these things—without a ton of in-person training. And if ServiceTitan is achieving its goal, it's giving technicians the visual price book and integrated financing they need to become good communicators and salespeople in the field. It's also creating the ability for techs to constantly be refining their skills. For example, ServiceTitan has a training content portal built into the technicians' mobile app. In between jobs, when they have five minutes to catch their breath in the truck, techs can watch training videos on better communications, how to present options, how to push and present memberships, or how to install a new piece of equipment that you now sell.

Automating as Much of the Business as Possible

After so many years of doing this, what motivates me to keep going are the contractors I work with. They're all salt-of-the-earth, amazing, hardworking people, but that's kind of the problem. They have to work *so hard*. It's crushing to see how many hours they put into their businesses and how they have to fight to put the same fires out day after day. The common advice that people give them is, "You've got to pull yourself out of that and work *on* the business instead of *in* the business."

But that is so freaking hard to do when there are so many problems—problems that, if left unsolved, can crush your business. That's why automation is so important. You're never going to be able to step away from working in the business unless you automate away the problems, and the only way to automate away the problems is with technology. There's just no other way, and I like to think that's where ServiceTitan helps. We automate so many of the industry's best practices so owners and their teams no longer have to work as hard manually. Now they can step back, work on the business, focus on the more high-value tasks and opportunities, make more money, have more profit, and grow.

The Best Way to Do Everything

There's a "best practices" way of doing certain things—how you schedule, how you dispatch, and how you sell in the field are good examples. There are many ways to do all of those things, but some of those ways are better than others.

To make sure we get it right, we talk to a lot of people. We strive to understand not only how they do something, but also why they do it that way and how effective it is. Then, we pick what we think is the most effective way and build that into the software. That "most effective way" is then pretty much the only way the software supports. If there too many different ways to do something it confuses the average user, who doesn't know what the right way is or which way they should go.

We are also releasing updates all the time—every month. For every change we make, we have to test the impact of that change on every function. So, for example, if there were 100 different ways to book a job, we would have to test all 100 ways to ensure the system would continue to work for our users.

Over time we have realized we cannot support everyone's desires, even though we really want to. But if we did that, our software would suck and our business would die!

We know now we have to identify the *best* way to do everything, and then that's how we build it. We have identified the absolute experts in their areas, such as Darius Lyvers for financing and Jaime DiDomenico for service agreements. We talk to them to figure out how to do that one thing really well.

That said, there are certain things, like payroll, where we know it's probably a battle we're not going to win. We're not going to be able to get everyone to pay their techs on the same commission system, so we have to build flexibility into the product, but we can only do that in a handful of areas.

The Importance of One App

As a home service business owner, you are in an on-demand response industry, which means you don't have time. Customers call you, and you've got to get the job done immediately. You don't have time to fumble through different apps to find the information you need.

Your tech in the field doesn't have time to look at one app and see all the customer's information, flip to another app, reenter all the data to create an invoice or estimate, flip to another app, reenter all the data again to get the customer processed and approved for financing, and then reenter all the data into yet another app to send a review request. That duplicate, triplicate, or multiplicate data entry kills you, and the time lag ruins your customer experience.

So we have to eliminate all of that. The only way to do it is by having all of those things in one app.

We also built our own scheduling, financing, marketing, sales, and other functionality into the app. Up until we built it, the other substitutes were not good enough. If, for example, there was a world-class inventory system for home services, we would probably acquire it and then build it into our product or integrate into it, but it just doesn't exist. Hence, we've had to build everything on our own. That's very expensive for us, but it's what we think the industry deserves, and we've made the investment.

Cost-Benefit Analysis

For anyone who is concerned about the cost of a technology like ours vs. the benefits, I would ask them several questions: What's the value of helping a tech or a comfort advisor increase their close rate by a few percentage points? What's the value of helping them increase their average ticket by several dollars? What's the benefit of having your CSRs book a higher percentage of appointments? What's the benefit of reducing your cancellations by some amount when you're spending tens of thousands or hundreds of thousands or even millions of dollars on marketing? What's the benefit of knowing which marketing programs work and which don't and being able to optimize how many leads you generate as a result of that?

If you make a five percent improvement in any one of those areas, that improvement alone pays for ServiceTitan.

Now, the thing is, most of our customers get that five percent improvement in *each* one of those areas, and when you compound five percent 10 times, that is a huge increase in their overall sales. That's typically complemented by also automating a lot of work-flows to reduce overhead, which means you benefit and profit from both sides—from an increase in sales *and* a reduction in cost.

Success Stories

Most of our biggest success stories are not from the largest companies, although those guys clearly benefit tremendously and make millions of dollars. It's from the smaller companies. I'm thinking of WyattWorks Plumbing in Ohio.

When he bought ServiceTitan, the owner, Andy Wyatt, told me he was making $600,000 a year. One year later, he called me back and said, "Ara, I just wanted to let you know, I just broke a million. I'm celebrating with my family, and I thought about all the things that helped me get here. You and ServiceTitan were one of the top things, and I just wanted to call you and let you know." I told him, "Call me when you're at two." Exactly one year later, he called me and he was at $2 million.

In fact, the product made such a big impact in his life that he ultimately had someone else take over the business, and he joined us as a team member here at ServiceTitan. He now works on building new products to help his fellow contractors all over the country.

Another guy I think about is Josh Campbell at Rescue Air in Texas. When Josh brought on ServiceTitan, he was at about $1 million a year. Four years later, he's at $9.5 million. ServiceTitan didn't do all of this. Josh Campbell did it. Andy Wyatt did it. Tommy Mello did it. But I think all of them would say they bought ServiceTitan to help them grow, and it absolutely did. Most of these success stories are the little guys who for the first time could get their lives back.

Then there is Julie Gardner from Bergen Plumbing Heating Cooling in Iowa. When I asked her if she was coming to our annual user conference, Pantheon, she said, "Yes, but you might not recognize me. I have lost nearly 50 pounds. I've been able to take time off including two weeks away from the office in July. Our kids have also noticed that mom and dad are home a lot more. And my husband and I are no longer slaves to the business, but actually get to work *on* it instead of *in* it. None of that could have happened without ServiceTitan."

Future of ServiceTitan

While ServiceTitan currently supports only plumbing, HVAC, electrical, and garage door companies, we're open to exploring other industries. It will take something like what we had with Tommy Mello, where even if we don't understand an industry very well, the other person is extremely technologically sophisticated, hungry for growth, and looking for a better way of doing things and can guide us into that business. We are looking at roofing, pest control, and going into commercial, because today we're pretty much only in residential. From there, who knows where it'll go?

On another note, there are a lot of big players in this space—Google, Amazon, Yelp, and Facebook, to name a few. The big concern in the home service industry is, "What if those guys try and cut us out of the equation?" We've been working hard to educate these big players. If they want to create an on-demand home service economy, they're not going to do it without local home service businesses. They're going to have to do it in partnership with you, and we can be the technology through which they can make that happen. So far, what's public is that one of those partners is Yelp, but hopefully soon there will be more partnerships with other goliaths in the industry.

Visit homeservicemillionaire.com/crm for more information about how ServiceTitan can help you grow your business faster while restoring some of your free time.

Once you have a CRM in place, you will have the data required to operate your business using key performance indicators (KPIs). Here's how they work.

Maximizing Business Performance with KPIs

Goals allow you to answer the question "Are we there yet?" An example of a goal is, "I want $5 million in revenue this year." If you are at $5 million, you are there. If not, you're not. Pretty simple.

What goals *don't* tell you is how the trip is going. Goals don't tell you if you'll ever get to your destination given your current route either. Goals *are* the destination.

Key performance indicators (KPIs) are like the dashboard in your car. The gauges tell you if you've got enough fuel and oil and how fast you're going. The GPS tells you whether you're on course and if there's traffic or an accident ahead so you can reroute.

KPIs allow you to stay on top of how your business is doing, so if you see something bad start to happen you can make adjustments quickly. KPIs allow you to see what's going on with key parts of the business so you can constantly be optimizing.

I know what you're thinking. "Key performance indicators? That sounds like corporate gibberish. How is that going to help me? Why should I care?"

Glad you asked.

Big businesses use KPIs to make sure they stay on course. So if you own a smaller business that you want to grow big and profitable, you'll definitely want to take advantage of this big-business tool.

There are dozens of KPIs you *could* be monitoring. The numbers you keep track of will vary depending on the function, i.e., operations will have one set, finance another, the warehouse yet another. I like to look at numbers in sets, because everything that happens from the initial call or form fill through the completed job is interconnected.

You can probably already guess my favorite set of KPIs to monitor is related to marketing and sales. Why? Because that set, if you get it under control, will change your business for the better the fastest. In other words, managing KPIs will help you get to your revenue goal faster.

The Eight Marketing KPIs

There are eight numbers you need to keep an eye on:

1. Average ticket total
2. Percentage of appointments techs/consultants converted into sold jobs
3. Percentage of appointments set from calls/form fills
4. Cost to acquire each call/form fill

    From those four numbers you can calculate the following:

5. Total number of completed jobs required
6. Total number of booked appointments needed
7. Total number of calls/form fills needed
8. Total marketing budget required

The math to get there is kind of a pain, so to make it easy for you I've created a calculator that walks you through it. Visit homeservicemillionaire.com/kpi-calculator to find it. On that site, there's a long video where I talk about KPIs in general and then one short informational video for each of the fields.

You need to care about these numbers. Without them, you won't know what you really need to spend per year on marketing to:

1. Generate the number of leads (calls and form fills) required,
2. Book the number of appointments you need,
3. Make sure enough of them turn into sold jobs, and
4. Create the amount of revenue you desire.

I use this particular set of KPIs to gauge exactly how much I should be spending on marketing to achieve my revenue goals and to identify areas of improvement in call-booking rates and sales conversions that will allow me to spend less on marketing—with better results.

Now let's take a deeper dive into the numbers—in reverse order.

What the Numbers Mean: Your marketing budget is going to be spread out among a number of different marketing activities. Maybe some of it is Valpak, some is online ads, etc. I'll go into detail about some of these options in the next chapter.

Cost to Acquire Each Call/Form Fill: To optimize this number, you're going to want to look at each marketing activity you're doing and figure out how many calls or form fills each one is driving, so you can figure out how much each call is costing you per campaign. That will allow you to understand what's working so you can spend more on it and less on what's not performing as well.

Percentage of Appointments Set from Calls/Form Fills: This number reflects how responsive your CSRs are. This is where it all starts. Unless your CSRs answer those phone calls within three rings and respond to those form fills within two to three minutes, I promise you that lead will move on to someone else—your competitor. The same is true if you are running chat or telling people to send you a text. Platinum response times are table stakes in the home service business.

Percentage of Appointments Techs/Consultants Converted into Sold Jobs: For appointments converted into sold jobs, you're tracking each tech that goes out to an appointment to see how many jobs he closed, meaning how many he actually confirmed and collected money on. It's one way of tracking his performance.

Average Ticket Total: For average ticket, you want to look at a few things:

1. Which technicians are doing better?
2. Who is collecting the most money?
3. How are they collecting the money?

This is another way of gauging their performance. Here's where it gets really interesting. Let's say you have a technician who is collecting $1,000 per call (two-and-a-half times the average of $400), but he's only closing one out of every two calls, which is a 50 percent close rate. That means his average ticket is $500. On the surface that looks OK. It's $100 more than your average call, after all.

But here's why that closing rate is actually a big problem. It's called opportunity cost.

Think about it. If a tech is only closing half the jobs, that means another company is getting the other half. Every failed close is costing you an opportunity to place your sticker on the product and get a good customer review, along with any referrals or recurring maintenance business to be had in the future.

So you're better off having a tech with a high close rate and then working with him on getting his ticket totals up over time.

KPI Exercise

Go to homeservicemillionaire.com/kpi-calculator and watch the video where I take you through the KPI exercise. Then input the dummy numbers below into the calculator to see how this works.

Let's say you want to make $5 million in revenue this year. How are you going to get there? Marketing. Lots of it.

But how much should you be spending on marketing to get $5 million in revenue? Answer: it depends on your KPIs. Answer: a lot more than you think. Got the calculator up? Good. Let me give you an example so you understand how it works:

1. **How much revenue you want (your goal):** Enter $5,000,000.
2. **Average ticket total (sales and service):** Enter $400 (which is the average ticket total in the garage door business).
3. **Percentage of appointments techs/consultants converted into sold jobs:** Enter 80 percent. (By the way, an 80 percent booking rate is really good. The average booking rate in the home service industry is more like 45 percent. So there's a chance your number might be nearer to average, at least at the beginning.)
4. **Percentage of appointments set from calls/form fills:** Enter 80 percent.
5. **Cost to acquire each call/form fill:** Enter $100.

Now look at the calculator and find out the truth about how many appointments you actually have to book and how much money you have to spend on marketing to get your $5,000,000.

1. **Total number of completed jobs** required is 12,500.
2. **Total number of booked appointments** required is 15,625.
3. **Total number of calls/form fills** required is 19,531.
4. **Overall marketing budget required** is $1,953,100.

Let that sink in.

Here's the thing: if your KPIs are optimal, you'll spend less on marketing! If your KPIs are crappy, you'll have to spend a lot more on marketing to get to your goal. And there will be less left in the bank to put in your pocket (i.e., profit) when all is said and done.

Now that you know how KPIs work, if you have accurate numbers from a CRM system, go ahead and plug in your numbers and see how you're doing.

Accurate Data Is Essential: Warning: If you don't have accurate numbers, get a CRM system in place first. Do *not* wing this. Guessing will not cut it and could hurt you more than help you. Accurate data is essential to making the right decisions that will lead to success. Get a decent CRM system in place and operational first so you are working with accurate numbers.

Calculating Customer Acquisition Cost (CAC): In addition to knowing what it is costing you to drive each inbound call and form fill, you need to know what it is costing you to actually *acquire* each new customer. At A1 Garage, knowing and controlling our customer acquisition cost (CAC) has been a huge factor in our success. That number is actually the sum of three separate numbers. (If you have a decent CRM system in place, determining these numbers should be pretty easy.) Here are the three costs that make up CAC:

1. **Lead-generation cost:** The cost of finding a new qualified lead via marketing, advertising, or cold calling. It includes the cost to acquire inbound calls and form fills, among other things. A lead is someone you believe would be interested in your product or service and has the ability to buy it.

2. **Cost to convert a qualified lead into a prospect:** The cost of turning that qualified lead into a prospect. A prospect is someone who reaches out to you and hopefully agrees to a sales appointment. Costs include marketing and advertising.

3. **Cost to convert a prospect into a customer:** The cost of converting that prospect into a customer. This includes discounting the price, throwing in extra services to add value to get the business, etc.

The arithmetic on this one is simple. Add 1, 2, and 3 and that is your customer acquisition cost. To improve this number, work on making your marketing, advertising, and sales efforts better and more efficient. Here are five tips you can use to start getting control of your CAC today:

1. Figure out where customers driving the most revenue are coming from and concentrate on acquiring more of that type of customer.

2. Invite your existing customers to spread the word about what a great home service provider you are via social media and neighborhood platforms, such as Nextdoor or Facebook.

3. Do whatever it takes to retain existing customers by sending occasional correspondence (birthday greetings are nice) and through service contracts that allow you to reconnect with the customer annually.

4. Put technology like ServiceTitan into place, which allows you to monitor what it is costing to acquire ideal customers so you can do more of what is working and less of what isn't.

5. Improve your presence on platforms such as HomeAdvisor so you can maximize the impact of those marketplaces.

PPT: The Three Elements of Business Success

There are three elements that must work in harmony if you're going to be successful in a home service business today. They are people, processes, and technology.

People

The first element is people. To optimize your organization, you're going to need your employees to change the way they are doing things. The problem is people *hate* change. So how do you get around this problem?

Get Buy-In: The answer is to involve them in the process. You need their buy-in, and they need to feel some ownership of the new idea. The key is to avoid a "top-down" approach where you are dictating every change and expecting them to snap to it. Stand in their shoes for a minute and ask, "What's in it for me?" Rather than giving orders, ask questions: "What's causing this issue?" "What in our process causes this to happen?" "What do you think we need to do to fix it?"

Once everyone agrees on the change, it's your job to make sure they follow through and go in the right direction. For example, if someone insists on doing things the old way, you can bring them into your office and say, "Didn't you and all your colleagues agree to do it this new way?"

Provide Training: Employees will need training on the processes. Bear in mind most people are visual, so videos are the way to go.

Note: Training videos are in addition to, not instead of, written operating manuals. They don't replace turning the screwdriver and other required hands-on training. Keep videos short and to the point, two minutes if possible and no longer than 12 minutes. According to a

2016 Wistia study, engagement drops off significantly after two minutes and then drops again after 12 minutes. So break longer videos into two or three parts if you can.

The other benefit of shorter videos is they are easier to create, which means they are more likely to get created! My general manager, Adam, produces several videos a week on different processes that we do and then stores them in a library on YouTube.

The added benefit of making these videos and putting them on YouTube is that Google loves them, so they'll show up in a search. We have one video on how to do a garage door spring replacement that has more than 1.5 million views!

Processes

When it comes to processes, there is no shortage of things you *could* do to improve your company. There is, however, a shortage of time. You know what I'm talking about. So you'll need to prioritize. Here are five things you can do to improve your processes right away.

1—Commit to Continuous Improvement: The first question is how big is the pain point? Let's say a key process now takes one hour. You know if you stop what you're doing and take a day to fix it that one-hour task will become a five-minute task. Move that one to the front of the line. (For a great way to think about continuous process improvement, check out the book *2 Second Lean* by Paul Akers.)

The most important thing is to commit to continuous improvement, no matter how miniscule. Even adding some simple checklists will make a big difference.

We are using Trello, but Basecamp, Zoho, Wunderlist, or even a Google document would work. The platform doesn't matter as much as having a list of tasks that need to be done on every call, which people can use to check off what they have completed.

2—Visit Other Businesses: Another strategy we use to improve processes at A1 Garage is inviting other home service professionals to tour our facility and then asking them for feedback on our company. For example, Cory, the owner of a successful roofing company in Minnesota, recently visited our office. He was very excited about what he took away from the visit and complimentary about everything we had going on.

I said, "That's great and thank you. Now give me some negative feedback." He said, "Well, I noticed you guys have about 10 different shirt colors and there was no one at the front desk to greet me. Those are two things I make sure of in my company." "Great," I said. "Anything else?" Cory said, "Well, since you're so close to the airport, why don't you do something with lights on the roof of your building so that when people fly over they see A1 Garage or A1Garage.com?"

I didn't think about the message different-colored shirts and not having anyone at reception was sending, and I never would have thought to put lights on the roof to advertise in a million years.

Ask your visitors: "Where do you think we are strong and weak? What opportunities in the marketplace do you think we're missing? What is going on outside our company that could take us out if we don't recognize it and take steps to prevent it?"

Invite professionals to visit your company and make it OK for them to give you constructive criticism. Why? Because if they are saying it, you know others are thinking it too. And you just might get a new idea that will make a big difference in your business.

The other thing we do at A1 Garage is make time to visit other businesses to see how they do things. And not just in Arizona. We fly all over the country to tour companies we think are doing great things, and we get tons of new ideas for how to improve our business this way. And if the host company wants constructive feedback from us, we're happy to return the favor. (Sometimes they don't, and that's OK too.)

We try to do this with companies we know at least once a month, and about every six months we'll find a new place and set up a visit.

3—Outsource Your Physical Inventory: I also recommend that you outsource your physical inventory. A1 Garage has a huge warehouse full of doors, materials to build doors, springs, etc. We used to do our own inventory and everyone hated it. I finally got sick of the complaining and hired inventory specialists RGIS. It's amazing. They can send as many "auditors" as you need, armed with wireless scanners to count, and they are fast and accurate. And because everything is electronic, they send me the inventory report as soon as they're done.

Optimizing your business is an ongoing process. Meet frequently with your managers and staff to find out what's not working and make a prioritized list of projects to solve the biggest problems. For more information about outsourced physical inventory, visit homeservice millionaire.com/inventory.

4—Look into Leasing Rather Than Buying Trucks and Equipment: To find out more details on leasing trucks and equipment vs. buying everything, I interviewed several experts. The general consensus on whether it's better to lease or buy is—it depends.

First, leasing has changed a lot. It used to be "open ended," where at the end of the lease term—say three years—the leasing company would tell you what they thought the vehicle was worth and then you were responsible for selling it and paying off the leasing company. The problem with that process was sometimes the number the leasing company gave was more than what you could get at auction so you were stuck paying the difference.

The way it usually works now is the buyout is predetermined and you have some choices. You can either turn the vehicle in and walk away, buy it and keep running it, or buy it and try to sell it for a profit. Some leases also offer a "gas and go" option where the payment includes oil changes and tire rotation. There are also extended service plans.

Here's what I think about leasing.

If you have a small operation, I'd go the cheapest way possible. If you've only got five guys, buy certified used vehicles and make them look good by wrapping them. Focus your resources on marketing to grow your business.

If you're a bigger company, leasing can be an advantage because having newer trucks on the road means the trucks have the newest technology, project a better image, and probably won't have maintenance issues beyond the basics.

Consider what you can afford and sustain in the long term. You don't want to get in over your head. For smaller companies, maybe it's mix and match—three leases for the heavily used trucks and two used, for example.

That said, in many situations there are some big advantages to leasing with new tax reform laws that allow you to write off assets rapidly. How much you can write off varies depending on the type of vehicle and equipment (and this varies from year to year). The tax savings can be pretty substantial depending on your situation. To find out more about your options, talk to your tax accountant and check out homeservicemillionaire.com/savings.

5—Get an Assistant: If you are struggling to keep up with email, missing appointments, or having problems keeping track of the status of all the projects in your company, you need to hire an assistant. Right now.

My productivity has *tripled* since I hired an assistant. Those details I listed above? They are all now handled by my assistant. She filters through my emails and makes sure I see the important ones as soon as possible. She also manages my calendar and chases me down to make sure I don't miss any appointments. Now that I'm no longer bogged down with those details, I have a lot more time to focus on running my business.

I repeat: get an assistant. Seriously. It'll change your life.

Technology

Finally, with the volume of data even a small business has to manage today having the right technology tools in place is critical to success. Here are seven key factors to consider when searching out and evaluating a technology tool:

1. Think long term. Your business is going to grow. Will this tool scale to accommodate an increase in staff? What about an increase in your customer base? Will it work as well when you have 400 to 500 employees as it does now with 40 or 50?

2. Consider your people. Is the tool user friendly and intuitive? Will it be easy to train on? Does it lead or follow industry standards for what it is (e.g., ServiceTitan for CRM)?

3. Consider the developer and the platform the tool is built on. Does it come standard with at least 80 percent of what you need? Avoid tools that are basic and whose salespeople offer the ability to customize. It sounds good, but it's expensive. Plus, every time the program is updated you have to go back and update all that custom code. Stick to the most trusted players in the category.

4. Commit to implementing technology properly and in a timely manner. There is nothing worse than spending a ton of money on a platform only to have it sit there for months unused because there's no one in charge of making sure it's rolled out. Hire an outside technology project manager to shepherd the rollout if necessary.

5. Make sure whatever system you are considering is capable of

hooking into whatever other systems are needed to work, such as your bank, parts vendor, or manufacturer (i.e., a compatible application programming interface, or API).

6. Investigate pricing structures. Some companies will charge for every minor upgrade.

7. Finally, ask how well the software company is funded. This is important because the last thing you need is to spend thousands on implementation just to have the company—and its support team—disappear the following year.

STOP: Five Things You Need to Fix Right Now

1. Create organizational charts and operating manuals and share them with your employees so they know what their responsibilities are and what you expect.

2. Get a CRM system in place. If you already have one but aren't using it, hire someone to help you roll it out and start following up on all those missed opportunities. If you're a residential plumbing, HVAC, electrical, or garage door service business and you can swing it, use ServiceTitan. Otherwise, check out another contractor business software, such as Housecall Pro.

3. Through KPIs, figure out how much you need to spend on marketing to achieve your revenue goals and start fixing the problems that are driving up the amount of marketing you need to do.

4. Get a handle on your CAC so you can spend less to get more new customers.

5. Inventory your people, processes, and technology—and make a plan for maximizing the impact of each. ▶▶▶

CHAPTER 3

GROWTH MACHINE

Y ou can have the greatest home service business on the planet, but if no one knows about you, you won't last long. Smart, aggressive marketing is the key to building a successful home service business. Be prepared to spend a serious amount of time and money on marketing if you want your business to succeed.

We both know there's no shortage of marketing advice out there, and most of it is unusable or just plain bad. What I'm about to share with you are the marketing strategies and tactics I've used to build my multimillion-dollar empire.

Your Ideal Customer

Before you do any marketing at all you need to understand what kind of customer you want to attract—your "ideal" customer.

Do you really want customers who take ages to make a decision or who only care about price? (I didn't think so.) You want the ones who care more about the quality of your job and your excellent communication and who are willing to pay a premium for your fast, 24-hour service. Right?

If you've had a great customer or two, write down everything you know about them.

Find Out Where They Hang Out

Now that you know who your ideal customer is, you need to figure out where they hang out. This doesn't have to be complicated. You've probably already had a few ideal customers. Why not contact them and do a short customer survey? Here are a few questions you could ask:

1. Where did you first hear about us?
2. Do you listen to podcasts or read any blogs? Which ones?
3. Are you on social media? If so, which platforms do you use the most?
4. When you were looking for a garage door service, where did you look first, second, and third?

Figure Out What They Want to Hear

When a prospective customer calls a home service expert, they are looking for a solution to a specific problem they are having. To create a marketing message they can connect with you need to understand two things:

1. What would motivate them to say yes and spend money on your service?
2. What kind of pain are they trying to kill (e.g., no more bugs in the house) or pleasure are they seeking (e.g., clean pool to swim in) by engaging your service?

My ideal client's house is an extension of their personality, so in addition to making sure the garage doors work properly they also need to look nice. Once I understood that, it was easy to dial in the right message.

Once you have a clear picture of your ideal customer and what you need them to believe about you (i.e., your "message"), you can put together a plan for reaching them.

For example, I recently advertised with Valpak, a direct-marketing company that provides print, mobile, and online advertising solutions and coupons. I selected Sun City, Arizona, the famous retirement community, and decided to microtarget the older community in one area.

In the ad, I showed a retired couple hugging one another in front of the "Welcome to Sun City" sign in the community. I included generous senior discounts and described the local community certifications that our target demographic cares about. I also showed us working on a retired gentleman's door, with him in the picture.

The results were spectacular. For a $150 campaign on Valpak, we produced more than $3,000 in returns in that one area—six times what we had been doing in that same area for the past 10 years. That's the power of the right message for the right demographic.

Be Honest with Them

Don't create false expectations in the mind of your customer. That means no deceptive marketing or bait-and-switch tactics. No phony cards that claim, "Your system's warranty is expiring. Call now!"

The goal is not a quick sale for short-term dollars; it's the opportunity to create a profitable long-term relationship with a happy customer that is based on satisfying a real need.

Brand and Branding

Your *brand* is how others perceive you. *Branding* is the image you show to your customers through everything they come into contact with—your trucks, website, Facebook page, business cards, uniforms, stationery, advertising, brochures, and you.

If you're on a tight budget, the two places you should spend money on first are your personal appearance and your trucks.

Uniforms and Wrapped Trucks

Our employees all wear golf shirts with the A1 Garage Door Service logo on them. They are available in black and red, our company colors.

And all our trucks are wrapped. I love wrapped trucks. In fact, I love them so much I bought a company that wraps cars and trucks! Wrap. Your. Trucks. Why? Because wraps make your trucks into free rolling billboards! They also allow you to do what's called "parketing." Parketing is advertising by parking your wrapped van or truck in a lot next to a high-traffic area.

A chimney repair company owner I worked with *tripled* his average ticket total by wrapping his trucks, getting an amazing new uniform, and improving his sales presentation.

Note: When looking for someone to wrap your trucks, you want someone who does everything—the printing, the laminating, etc.—and has control over the whole process. Ask for referrals, and then be sure to check the quality of the materials and installation.

Website and Facebook Page

You'll also need a website and a company Facebook page. The website is its own animal and you should hire a good developer who specializes in home service websites to help you.

Be clear about what you offer. At the very least, put the phone number in big, bold numbers and exactly what you do at the top of the page—Garage Door Repair. Follow with a single, strong call to action, such as, "Call now for a free estimate." I am also a big believer in videos because they give the customer a feel for the company and build trust.

Facebook is important for your business because your customers are there, guaranteed. A company page gives you a presence and allows people looking for your home service offering to find you. It also allows your customers to easily refer you to their Facebook friends. You'll need to add new content to the page about every other week to keep it fresh. Content can be as simple as posting a video or an article that is helpful to your customers.

There's a ton of stuff you can do with your company page, and Facebook is adding new features all the time. For example, I created a commercial that plays in the header. You can check it out at facebook.com/A1GarageDoorService.

The other reason you need a company Facebook page is to do advertising and to recruit for your business. We'll talk more about both of those things a little later in the book.

While you're getting that stuff into place, you'll want to build your reputation in the area by getting as many positive customer reviews on popular review platforms as possible.

Building Your Reputation Online

Four Review Platforms You Must Be On

The mission of review sites—and there are dozens of them—is to match a consumer with the right service contractor. There are four review platforms that, as a home service business, you absolutely *must* be on. They are Yelp, Google Reviews, HomeAdvisor, and Angie's List.

Yelp: Yelp has a platform that allows your customers to leave reviews of your service that your prospective customers can use to make decisions about whether to hire you—or not. Yelp is also the review platform Google favors the most, apart from its own, Google Reviews.

In fact, A1 Garage's Yelp reviews come up higher in Google search results than the results from all the money I spend on organic search engine optimization (SEO) and pay-per-click (PPC) ads put together.

There is one small catch: Yelp reviews will come up higher than anything else on Google, *if* you receive enough reviews. I'll talk more about how generate a lot of reviews quickly later in this chapter.

Google Reviews: Your goal is to be among the "seven pack" (the top seven locations for your locale). Even if you're number five in that list, if you have more than a hundred five-star reviews, you're going to get calls.

Note: The more things customers discuss in the review, the more Google will find you for different searches. Encourage customers to talk about why they called, what parts they had installed, the benefits of installing those parts, etc. The longer the review, the better. There is no such thing as a too-long five-star review.

HomeAdvisor and Angie's List: I bet you already know HomeAdvisor and Angie's List are two other important review sites. But what you may not realize is the two companies have merged. They are now one publicly traded company called ANGI Homeservices.

The important thing for you to know is each platform continues to run as its own entity. That means customers who always looked to HomeAdvisor to find a home service provider are still using it, and Angie's List users are still using that site. To get in front of those prospective customers, you have to be in both places too.

In the old days, a customer couldn't see Angie's List reviews unless they paid for a membership. Today, they can see everything. And winning an Angie's List Super Service Award can really put your company on the map.

To find out more about how home service business owners could be successful on the HomeAdvisor platform, I sat down with its chief operating officer, Craig Smith. I opened by telling Craig that I used to have a dedicated person responding to HomeAdvisor leads. I had one of my customer service representatives (CSRs) download the HomeAdvisor app to her phone and instructed her to call a lead immediately when it came in. The deal was she got $5 for every call she booked off HomeAdvisor. We're on a different program now so we don't do this anymore, but if you're just getting started, it *really* works.

SUPERCHARGE YOUR HOME SERVICE BUSINESS

Craig Smith, COO, HomeAdvisor

It's so smart to have incentives in place for key behaviors that drive success on the platform. It's really important to call leads immediately. Our research shows that performance diminishes quickly after just *five minutes*. That's because at least two other providers may also be calling that customer.

Reviews are also very important. You have to be encouraging your customers to leave reviews all the time because recency matters. People will scroll back three to four months to see what the trends are, just like reviews for a restaurant. So if the last review you have up there was written in 2015 that could be a problem.

You also want to make sure your profile is fully populated and reflects a high level of professionalism. Include pictures of work that has been completed. Before-and-after shots are great, but make sure you include pictures of your crew too. People want to see who is coming to their home. List any awards and community involvement, and then make sure the CSR who answers or makes the call is an extension of that professionalism. If you do those things, it leads to a good outcome most of the time.

Common Mistakes

One common mistake we see with smaller companies is an unwillingness to invest in their business. To them, the HomeAdvisor membership is purely an expense item. A lot of people are content with word of mouth, but they don't realize there is an opportunity cost that comes with word of mouth—especially if the business it's driving is all from lower-margin neighborhoods. HomeAdvisor can help contractors attract higher-margin work, the work that makes people lots of money. But to get there you have to invest in some infrastructure.

Let's say your business gets a call, but it doesn't immediately turn into a job. Most people will let the lead drop and wait for another call. They don't realize they need to have a plan and people in place to maximize the potential of that call. What you need to be doing is sending an email or text to the prospective customer after the initial point of contact, and following up diligently a week later, even if the customer says they picked someone else.

What we know is that even if people say they're not accepting anymore quotes, sometimes they're not comfortable with the first point of contact or they're dissatisfied with that quote. They end up canceling and, as a result, are back out there looking. If you've followed up, there will be a level of familiarity, and there's a better chance you'll get a second chance at quoting that business.

Bigger businesses tend to struggle with how to scale and integrate HomeAdvisor with more traditional marketing designed to build brand awareness, bring repeat business, and stimulate word of mouth. For both small and large companies, the most important thing they can do is put business processes in place that result in great customer service, great sales service, and the ability to track cost vs. close rate relative to each other—and not just how many jobs the site is producing, but the quality of those jobs.

Increasing Positive Reviews

To get more positive reviews and feedback on HomeAdvisor, ask! I've hired many pros who are members of our marketplace to work on my home. Most don't ask me for a review at the conclusion of the job. All you need to say is, "I'd really appreciate it if you'd take the time to write a review for me." Just making that simple statement creates accountability with the customer and increases the chances they'll follow through.

You also want to ask for reviews at all touch points—your invoice, estimate, email signature, brochure, and website—wherever you are interacting with that customer. Then, make it really simple for people to give you that review. One of the easiest ways to do so is to send them a text link. This capability is included in your HomeAdvisor account. All you need to say is, "I am going to send you a text with a link where you can write a quick review." If it's easy for them to do, it's OK to ask them to actually complete the review in your presence.

If you haven't participated in the HomeAdvisor marketplace for a while, now is a good time to come back. The platform is getting better all the time. We now have the ability to track close rates by source, how a homeowner who finds us through TV ads converts into business from pro vs. affiliate, and the close rate cost of marketing for that source, which allows us to invest more in what is working. Everybody wins when close rates are high!

HomeAdvisor's goal is to help you grow your business and expand profitability by working smarter rather than harder. To learn more about how it can help, please visit homeservicemillionaire .com/marketplace.

How to Get a Flood of Five-Star Reviews

Be a Five-Star Home Service Provider: If you want five-star reviews, you have to be a five-star provider. That means you always give customers a little bit more than they expect.

A five-star review begins with the person who answers the phone. Have your CSR prime the pump for a good review by saying, "If you receive anything less than five-star service, please let me know."

Demonstrate that you value the customer's time by calling or texting them to let them know their technician is arriving in 15 minutes.

Once the technician completes the job and the customer has inspected the work, have the tech get a review from them on the spot. If the tech explains that the review is for them so they can improve, customers are way more likely to do it. The next day, follow up with the customer and make sure they are still happy with their service.

The point is, make sure you deliver your core service as expected, but also offer something more that will impress them and make them more likely to take the time to share that experience with others.

Jump-Starting Reviews: If you don't have a ton of reviews just yet, HomeAdvisor and Angie's List both offer ways to drive inbound calls and traffic to your website through advertising and the creation of special offers.

You can also run some Facebook ads to sell Yelp deals, and then ask those customers to leave a review on Yelp.

Customer Surveys: It's important to solicit *all* customers for reviews because most customers will not leave a positive review if they are happy. It's too much work!

On the other hand, you better believe unhappy customers *will* take the time to post a negative review. Research shows that when people have a bad experience with a contractor they tell an average of 22 people about it!

The best way to solicit great reviews and preemptively address bad ones is to provide every customer with a short survey immediately after their service has been completed. A survey will let you know who your happy customers are and give you the opportunity to get in front of the unhappy ones before they go online.

Provide customers with an incentive to take the survey, such as a discount on their next service call or a $10 gift card. Make it clear that as soon as they complete the survey, they'll receive an email with a link to download their gift.

Once you have some results, look for the very happy customers and give them a call. Thank them for taking the survey and ask them to tell you more about their experience. Once their experience has been validated, ask them if they'd mind taking some time to spread the word. If they say yes, send them an email with exact instructions on what you want them to do. Here is a sample:

Hi Mrs. Smith,

I was pleased to hear you were happy with the service we provided. We would love it if you'd help us spread the word by writing a review about our company. To make it easier for you, I've drafted a sample review based on our conversation. Feel free to use it as is or edit as you see fit. Links to the sites we belong to appear below. Thanks in advance for your time.

If you don't have very many reviews, ask all friends and family who have experienced your service to step up and leave you one. Invest the time to ask all your happy customers to leave you a review because the more reviews you have, the more reviews you'll get. That's just how it works.

Managing Negative Reviews

Negative customer reviews are a powerful opportunity to improve and serve the customer better. In fact, I've learned more about my business from the complaints than I have from the good reviews.

When you address negative customer reviews properly, word spreads. It shows that you care. Customers want to do business with people who care. They are very impressed when you call and offer to make things right for them.

I know personalized customer service like this doesn't scale, but it's what makes us better than our competitors. And that's why at A1 Garage we have more than 400 reviews on Yelp, with the vast majority of them totally positive.

Here is how to resolve a negative review in your business (I do this exact process every single time):

1. Reach out to the customer with a private message telling them that you care and want to make things better.
2. If they reply, get their phone number and explain that you would like to call and speak with them to further troubleshoot. (If they don't respond, do a database search and try to find their phone number.)
3. Once you have them on the phone, get them to vent first. Most unhappy customers just want someone to listen to them. Ask as many questions as you can, and then actively listen to everything they are saying. Empathize with them by saying things like, "I'm so sorry this happened to you."
4. After you have heard their story, fix it for them on the spot if at all possible. If you can't fix it immediately, tell them what you are going to do about their problem—and then do it. At the end of the call, thank them again for making time to talk, and reassure them that this will never happen again.

5. Finally, be sure to respond to the negative review publicly. Apologize and explain what happened and what you did or will do to fix it. Make sure the response comes from you, the business owner, because that shows readers of the review how serious you are about making things right. I always include my cell phone number, and guess what? It hardly ever rings. Adding the phone number reinforces the fact that I care and I'm accessible, which reassures prospective clients that if something should go wrong, it will receive my personal attention.

Apologizing in Person: You know that feeling you get when you know you've screwed up in your business?

Here's one incident I will always remember. It was in the fall of 2008, at the beginning of the recession, right as we were scrambling to get A1 Garage off the ground.

That day, one of my employees completely missed a customer's two-hour appointment window. The customer was fuming—and I knew that an over-the-phone apology wasn't going to cut it. I also knew it was just a matter of time before that angry customer would go online and tell everyone they knew how crappy we were. Being a young business that still needed to build a lot of trust with our customers, we could not afford *any* negative reviews!

I immediately grabbed my car keys and headed out the door. First stop: Starbucks for a gift card. Second stop: florist for a bouquet of flowers. Pretty soon I was standing on the customer's doorstep and ringing the doorbell.

The customer opened the door and was dumbstruck.

I said, "Hi, I'm Tommy Mello, the owner of A1 Garage. I'm so sorry we missed the appointment you booked with us—and I hope this gift card and the flowers make up for it. If you give us a second chance, I'll call one of our best technicians now to fix your problem."

We got the business, along with a nice write-up in the regional newspaper. Some people saw it as a PR stunt, but that was not the point. The point was our commitment to delivering the outstanding level of customer service we wanted to become known for—no matter what it took.

Google Guarantee

If you're running home service ads, Google has a new product you can apply for called Google Local Services. The ads display a small green "Google Guaranteed" shield next to your Google listing, which assures the customer that you're licensed, insured, and have been prescreened.

Google guarantees your customer will be satisfied with any job they book with you through its Local Services platform. If they are not satisfied, and they file a claim, Google will investigate and you'll have an opportunity to make it right with the customer. If a resolution is not worked out, Google will insure the work with a lifetime (per user) guarantee of $2,000. In fairness, Google also allows the contractor to dispute and request a refund for irrelevant or bad leads.

I believe Google Guarantee is going to elevate the home service industry and allow businesses that can pass muster to charge more and make more money. Darryl Margaux and Matt Glickman, cofounders of the search engine marketing company SearchKings, agree. According to Darryl, Google Guarantee will ultimately separate "the pros from the Joes" because to be eligible for the program your company must meet all of Google's requirements.

GETTING GOOGLE GUARANTEED

Darryl Margaux and Matt Glickman, Cofounders, SearchKings

Every employee you intend to send on a Google Guarantee job has to undergo a Pinkerton background check. Here's the thing: it's pass/fail. So if just one employee you included on the application fails that background check, the whole company fails. And once your company fails, it is very difficult to get approved. There is an appeal process, but it is very unlikely that a failed company will pass on appeal.

Let's say you have a great tech who made a dumb mistake 10 years ago that involved a violent crime, property theft, or a home offense. You decided to overlook it when you hired them, but you know it will come up in their background check. You will need to either take a chance and declare it to Pinkerton or leave that employee off the program application, which means you won't be able to send that person out for leads that were generated through the Google Local Services platform.

To expedite approval, make sure you take time to understand the process and get organized. The process begins with the background check. Google brings in a third party to facilitate this process and ensure privacy. The business owner submits their license, insurance, and both a personal and company background check. Field technicians submit their social security number and date of birth and disclose any convictions. Once Google receives the information from Pinkerton, that's when it begins its approval process.

If everything is in order, the approval can go through the system in one to four weeks. If things aren't in order, that's when it can drag on. Once you clear Pinkerton, someone will actually come to your office—which can't be located in your home, by the way. They'll look at your building insignia and your vehicles, which must be wrapped. They'll take note of the license plates, and they'll get in your trucks and start them up.

If you don't get everything perfect, Google isn't going to pick up the phone and let you know. And you aren't necessarily going to know how to get to the right person at Google to figure out what is holding things up. It can be something as simple as a tech not providing all of the requested information. SearchKings has all those contacts and we know the process, so we can help a company get unstuck. We can also help guide a company from the start to make sure everything gets through the system successfully the first time.

If you're interested in finding out more about how SearchKings can help you with Google Guarantee, check out homeservicemillionaire.com/google-guaranteed.

Amazon Home Services

You might think of Amazon solely as a place to buy products, but it's actually a great place to grow your home service business because you can now list, refer, and book jobs through Amazon Home Services.

Amazon is a mammoth marketplace. Amazon.com alone attracts 2.6 billion visitors a month, and it's the third-largest search engine after Google and YouTube! It is also the only platform that serves up and sells products (and now services) based on purchase behavior. It gives you direct access to Amazon Prime members—more than 100 million of them with credit cards on file, ready to purchase.

Here's how it works. Amazon matches buyers with related services and notifies you of service opportunities in your area in real time. For example, let's say a customer purchases a showerhead. Amazon will ask if they want to upgrade to the installation purchase. It's like having a 24-hour booking agent available—for free. The Amazon Home Services app then alerts you when a job is available to claim, and no money is involved until the job is booked, sold, and performed.

Similar to Google Local Services, Amazon Home Services requires background checks, general liability insurance, and current licensing for trade professionals such as electricians, plumbers, HVAC specialists, general contractors, and more. You can opt to sell prepackaged services—such as TV wall mounting, bed or treadmill assembly, move-in or move-out house cleaning—or recurring services. Amazon deducts the fees as a percentage of the service price, excluding any taxes collected through the website.

When it comes to growing your home services business, a presence on Amazon is now just as important as a presence on Google. Take the time to find out more about this program. You don't want to be left behind. For more information about how Amazon Home Services can help grow your business, visit homeservicemillionaire.com/Amazon.

Social Media

Social media can be an effective way to raise awareness of your company, but it takes a lot of time to do well and recoup your investment. I already touched on Facebook and I'll talk even more about it in the next chapter. In the meantime, here are the other platforms you should consider.

Craigslist: Craigslist is a website that provides local classified ads and forums for jobs, housing, items for sale, personals, services, and local community events. Organized both by region and by city, Craigslist connects buyers and sellers in more than 300 communities.

You can post an ad to Craigslist under the services section, which is further broken down by different types of services. Posting to different sections will allow your ad to be seen by a wider audience of people who may be looking for your services.

You can also test different cities or regions to gauge where there is the most interest for your type of product or service.

Maybe you hate Craigslist.

I don't. I love it, and here's why.

I started my garage door business during the run-up to the Great Recession. After I finished each job, I would post an ad on Craigslist and from that ad I would get three or four jobs a day. Through Craigslist, I met more home flippers, property managers, and real estate agents than I could have almost any other way. Even though it was a cheaper customer base, they tended to use us often and they told other people about us. In that way, they were the best customers possible because referrals are the best advertising.

Craigslist prohibits advertisers from overposting or spamming their users. That's OK. Just learn the rules and follow them. You'll still get excellent exposure.

Neighborhood Sites: You're also going to want to join your local Facebook and Nextdoor groups. You want to be wherever people are asking their neighbors for referrals. Assign someone to monitor those groups for people asking for referrals and direct them to respond to those requests as soon as possible.

Coupon Sites: At A1 Garage, we do a ton of business with AAA, Amazon, Groupon, and other sites that offer good coupons for users. We also do heavy marketing on our mailer sites, such as Valpak and Money Mailer. (I'll talk more about direct mail later in this chapter.)

Here's what we found with deal sites. They allow you to get your foot in the door. Once you get in there, nine times out of 10 there are more problems than the customer realizes because chances are whatever it is that is broken—garage door, AC unit, plumbing, etc.—hasn't been looked at in a very long time. We have gone out to do $39 tune-ups and ended up selling new doors based on the poor condition of the original door. You just never know what is going to happen on that first call.

Even if it turns out to be just a tune-up, it gives us a chance to put our sticker on the door and offer the customer an annual service plan to keep the door working properly. I might not make any money on that $39 tune-up, but I will in the future because I know they will call us to service that door for as long as it makes sense. And once it needs to be replaced, I know we'll be the ones to do that too.

Note: I never sign exclusive deals that prohibit me from using other deal sites for a year. That policy started with Groupon to combat the copycat deal sites that sprouted up after they got hot. I always refuse to sign those things, and somehow they still find a way to work with me—and I bet they will for you too.

Dominating Search

Destination: Google Page 1

Google wants to serve up sites to you and your prospective customer that it thinks will deliver the most value and help you solve your problem. When your customers search for your home service on the internet, they *must* find your website. If they don't, you're done. You need to strive to be on the first page of search results. Why? Because the higher your site is ranked on the results page, and the more frequently a site appears in people's search results, the more visitors it will receive—visitors who can then be converted into customers.

Search Engine Optimization (SEO)

You can help Google determine whether your site should be placed on the first page of someone's search results by optimizing your website through a practice called search engine optimization (SEO). The main goal of SEO is to improve the visibility of your website or a webpage in a search engine's unpaid results—often referred to as "natural," "organic," or "earned" results.

Searchers (your prospective customers) won't find your company unless you have content on your website or in your articles that exactly matches the key words they type into the search. For example, if someone wants a new garage door, they will type "new garage door" into the Google search field. These three words are the exact key words that Google will look for, and it will return the websites that best fit the person's query.

Most people end up searching for the same key words. In my industry segment, typically customers search for "garage door repair + city name." That is why when you begin to type something, Google often wants to autofill the rest of it. It has deep insights into what everybody is searching.

Key word optimization is a whole science unto itself. We A/B test all our key words to determine our return on investment for certain search terms. It works, but it can get expensive pretty quick.

Note: SEO is a beast. The rules change almost daily. You need to find a professional you can trust who eats, lives, and breathes SEO and understands the home service industry. We can help point you in the right direction. Visit homeservicemillionaire.com/SEO for a free evaluation.

Low-Hanging SEO Fruit—Google Citations: A Google citation is the name, address, and phone number—sometimes referred to as the "NAP" of your business—as Google finds it listed on the internet. If you are aiming for top page listings in Google Places, citations can help you gain a favorable position.

There are hundreds of citation sites out there. The goal is to be on as many as possible with your address and phone number (always the same) and as many pictures and as much information as you can possibly put on there.

There are niche-specific citation sites. Get on them and go ahead and pay for them if necessary, especially if they give you access to useful data.

You can turn Facebook and YouTube videos into citation sites as well. The more places you can put your business name, address, and phone number, the better.

I realize this section has been somewhat like drinking from a fire hose, but don't sweat it. You don't have to do everything right now. Look at your options and prioritize. Devote some time and resources to figuring out if the stuff you're already spending money on (SEO and PPC) is actually working. Then get the review machine going. Add in other things as soon as you can. For more information about Google Citations, visit homeservicemillionaire.com/citations.

Customer Referral Programs

Generating customer referrals needs to be part of your overall marketing plan. Calls to action for referrals should be embedded into all your marketing materials—ads, coupons, blogs, newsletters, and even employee email signatures—anything a current or past customer might come into contact with. Why?

More than 40 percent of A1 Garage's business comes from referrals from friends, family, or neighbors of happy customers who loved our service.

If you're doing great work, this referral process will occur organically. But you can accelerate the process a lot by creating a program that rewards your customer for spreading the word about your business.

To do that, ask customers to share their love for you on Facebook and local sites such as Nextdoor. Ask them to share pictures of your work on their personal Facebook page. (Before-and-after shots are the best.) You can also ask them to share on their local neighborhood Facebook and Nextdoor pages.

Here at A1 Garage, we offer our customers a $10 Starbucks gift card if they are willing to share their experience on Facebook, along with a couple of pictures of the installation. This is powerful because people feel much more comfortable hiring home service providers that others in their circle have used, especially providers those people liked well enough to take the time to share their experience. You can even provide them with a special code they can share with their circle for a free inspection.

Old School Is New Again

Digital is great and it is the future, but there are some old-school approaches that are still very effective.

Pick up the Phone

The most important thing you can do after the job is done is follow up. At A1 Garage, we have one person whose only job is to call customers a few days after the work is done to make sure the customer is happy. She then asks for a testimonial, a Facebook or Nextdoor share, and if it would be OK for the tech to stop by and put a sign in their front yard. The yard signs and shares on social media create instant credibility with other people in the neighborhood and generate a ton of referrals.

Direct Mail

Direct mail is not dead. Far from it. In fact, if you really want to get in front of a customer, a direct-mail campaign can be very effective. A 2015 neuroscientific study sponsored by the U.S. Postal Service Office of the Inspector General (OIG) found direct-mail ads to be superior to those viewed online across the board. The study said, "Digital ads seized the attention of consumers quicker, but physical ads held that attention longer, elicited a greater emotional reaction, and played a more direct role in ultimate purchase decisions."

To get a deeper dive on direct mail, I sat down with Mike Davis, chief executive officer of Valpak.

MAXIMIZING THE DIRECT-MAIL MOMENT

Mike Davis, CEO, Valpak

A recent study by McCann—agency of record for the U.S. Postal Service—found that the average American spends 25 minutes a day with mail. At a recent conference, McCann's CEO, Harris Diamond, described it this way: "You come home from work, the mail in one hand, the cell phone in your pocket, and you sit down to go through the mail. It's an important moment in people's lives and one that presents great marketing opportunities." Diamond called this the "Mail Moment."

So when, not if, that average American is in the market for home services, you want to make sure your company is a part of that daily ritual!

One way to achieve that goal is to send out individual pieces to your own mailing list. The problem with this approach is that most home service companies don't have huge lists, and if they do, they are limited to existing customers. The other problem is if you send anything larger than a four-by-six-inch postcard, each piece costs as much as a first-class letter (47 cents and up). That adds up pretty quickly. So what exactly do you put on that post-card to get the recipient to act?

To connect with existing and new customers more eco-nomically and effectively, it's better to partner with a direct-mail provider who has high brand awareness and is an expert in pro-moting home services. I know I'm biased, but I believe Valpak is that partner. Why?

Valpak has 91 percent brand awareness in U.S. households when it comes to finding home service providers both for home improvement and home repair. The great thing about Valpak is that we can get you in front of your ideal customer for about a tenth of what it would cost you to send them something yourself.

The key to success with Valpak is to pick the right zones, which we call NTAs or "neighborhood trade areas," based on your business. Our sales executives help dial that in. We also have an incredible amount of data we can look at and a big research and mapping team who can help. We usually recommend that you target the zones close by as well as some zones that have a certain demographic that trends toward higher ticket sales. If you have your own data or a mailing list, we can look at that too.

The next step is to figure out what your offer is. You can have more than one offer in an envelope depending on whether you're sending it to an existing customer you want to keep in the fold or a new prospect you want to incentivize to reach out. For example, if you're a security company, maybe one is for a system upgrade and the other is for a complete home solution. Our team can even help design the coupon if needed.

Valpak is incredibly effective, but it's not something you can do for a month or two and expect results. You really have to go into it knowing it's a 12-month commitment because we need time to test offers and pictures front and back, performance in five vs. 10 zones, etc. We need time to see what moves the needle for you and get you to a perfect Valpak mix. Our experience is that you need to *at least* break the five-month mark before you start gaining those valuable lifetime customers.

The other reason taking time is important is you want to be top of mind when people actually need your service. They might not need it the first time you show up in the mail, but if they keep seeing you, they will choose your brand over others when the time comes to hire someone for the job.

If, like most people, you're doing several different things to market your business and want to track what's coming from Valpak, we can provide you with a unique tracking number or discount code that can be unequivocally tracked to us. The other thing you can do during the two-week period around the mail drop is check to see if there is a spike in website traffic and if your search engine marketing campaign is generating more clicks and conversions.

Direct mail can be an incredibly effective way to nurture existing customers and find new ones, because in a world of screens, receiving mail that is not a bill and actually offers value is a welcome change.

To learn all the ways Valpak can help your home service business be more successful, visit homeservicemillionaire.com /direct-mail.

Radio, TV, and Billboards

Radio, TV, and billboards can be unbelievably effective—when you are already maxing out your other direct-response channels. My advice is do everything else first.

When you do decide to play, you want to make sure you have a clean message and your Google rankings are high.

Radio, TV, and billboards are about creating impressions that live in your customers' subconscious so when they see or hear something, they think, "Hey, that's the guy whose commercials and trucks we see all over the place."

It can be hard to directly track the results of these channels, but you should see increased results in your other media efforts if you're at it consistently for a decent length of time. To become top of mind, you really need to be doing it for a minimum of 90 days at a time. The frequency is what's going to drive your brand into someone's subconscious and create that ripple effect.

If you're doing a radio ad in particular, you want to be where people don't change the station. In my experience, country and talk radio are great, and sports channels do well too. Focus on owning an audience so you can get them to hear your spot seven to eight times during their drive instead of sprinkling spots all over the place.

For TV, I'm a big fan of prime time. If you're selling an expensive product, you want to make a longer commercial or infomercial where you have a chance to tell a story. Mondays and Tuesdays are the best days for home service businesses to be on TV.

Billboards can also be super effective. The problem is people tend to put too much stuff on them. Keep it simple. Do something that makes people think of your company. It can just be your company name—people will Google it later and find you. If you have a very good vanity website or phone number, you can use that (e.g., A1Garage.com or 1800JUNK). If you have a common phone number or a long web address, stick with the company name and what the company does.

Finally, don't try to do your own media buys. Find the biggest company in town and ask who they use. The reason is the local media company will be buying so much in your local area that they will get the best discounts, which they can then pass on to you.

Business Partnerships

Once your marketing is in place, the next step is to begin talking to other businesses and building collaborative relationships where you can use your marketing program and expertise to benefit both of you.

I've met with my garage door manufacturer in Ohio and my garage door opener manufacturer in China, along with numerous other suppliers, to establish relationships that have led to sweet deals for both of us.

Show these partners how many searches for their product are going to their competitors' sites instead of theirs. If you can get them to piggyback on your brand and expertise, you can drive business to their dealers in exchange for better pricing on components.

When you take advantage of opportunities to partner up with complementary businesses, everybody wins. ▶▶▶

CHAPTER 4

LEAD-GENERATION MACHINE

Driving Inbound Leads

Every sale begins with a lead. The main purpose of marketing is to generate lots of leads in a cost-effective and predictable way, which you and your technicians can then turn into happy customers.

I'll share three strategies that have worked well for me. First, Facebook ads are really underpriced for all industries, with leads costing around $4 to $8 each. That's cheap! I recommend you take advantage of Facebook ads now because it won't be this way forever. Serial entrepreneur and digital media expert Gary Vaynerchuk pointed this out using the example of how cheap Google AdWords were just five years ago. You could get a key word like "insurance" for a dollar. Then big businesses discovered how effective AdWords were and started dumping their massive ad budgets into it. Now the key word "insurance" costs $1,000 because the littler guys have to compete with the bigger wallets. Remember, you'll need to experiment until you find the right ads at the right price that work for your business. To cut the learning curve, you may want to hire a proven Facebook ad expert to guide you.

Next, I recommend partnering with a reputable lead-generation company because it will provide you with the leads; all you have to do is follow up. If you're a garage door service provider, check out homeservicemillionaire.com/leads.

And last, it is important to look at the bigger picture and focus on the lifetime value of every customer you bring in the door. Maybe you don't make any profit at all on the first visit; you just pay for your tech's time. As long as you didn't *lose* any money, you still won because you got your sticker on their garage door, and that customer will talk to their neighbors. And if you follow up, they might also sign a service agreement. As you look at your leads, you have to factor the lifetime value of those customers into the equation.

The best way for home service companies to generate leads, however, is to buy them. Marc Levesque is cofounder of Webrunner Media, an agency that specializes in lead generation for home service companies. I recently spoke with him to get his advice on everything from paid advertising and retargeting to driving inbound phone calls and crafting the perfect offer.

FIVE BEST WAYS TO GENERATE LEADS

Marc Levesque, Cofounder, Webrunner Media

Google AdWords

The fastest way for contractors to get leads is to dig into paid advertising, starting with search engines. Start with Google AdWords, which has the lion's share of the market. Then move to Bing. While Bing doesn't have the volume Google has, the quality is higher and there's not as much competition, which means the cost per lead is lower.

Google AdWords is good because it puts your company in front of people in your area who are searching for your service and ready to buy. Especially if there is not a lot of competition in your area, Google AdWords is an easy way to pull in people already interested in your service.

Facebook and Instagram

Facebook and Instagram are two other places you can generate a lot of leads. This is a longer-term strategy to make people aware of your service so when the need arises they will already be familiar with you and more likely to reach out. Once someone engages with your ad, you can start retargeting them (at a much lower cost) with a different kind of ad, image, or carousel slideshow.

Retargeting is the ability to serve ads on other sites to people who have previously visited your site. (If you've ever visited a retail site and noticed banner ads for that site suddenly appearing on other sites you visit, you've been retargeted.) Retargeting allows you to focus your advertising spend on people already familiar with your company who have recently demonstrated interest in your services.

The best results come from a combination of Google or Bing pay-per-click (PPC) advertising, plus Facebook and Instagram retargeting and display ads.

If someone told me they tried Facebook ads and they didn't work, I would ask them what they did exactly. Where most people go wrong is they go too narrow. They start right away by tagging interests in their campaign. They include all those modifiers because they want to save money. What they don't realize is they should go wide because people who are scrolling through the news feed are not going to stop and look at their ad unless they are interested.

Another problem is they don't know how to craft compelling ad copy and the visuals they use are usually too generic. They also don't give the campaign enough time to work. They spend $20 and nothing happens, so they get worried and shut it off.

I have a friend who spends $10,000 a month on Facebook ads. The key to his success is he understands the "traffic temperature." If he is marketing to a cold lead, that is one type of ad. If the person engages, that lead is now warmer so the ad they are shown changes. He is constantly testing ads, both messaging and creative. And because he is spending enough, he gets very good data about what is working and not working. If you are doing Facebook ads with a tiny budget, and you don't have experience to fall back on, you can't amass enough data to know what changes you need to make to be successful.

Use Landing Pages

To drive inbound calls, use a landing page. Whatever kind of campaign you're running—traditional, print, radio—you want to send potential customers to a location where the action you want them to take is the only option they have. If you send them to your website, they can get lost. A landing page should list the exact benefit of why they should call you, with an incentive for them to take action and options to reach out through a form, live chat, phone call, or even text. Text is really up and coming.

Create a Compelling Offer

The next thing you need is a compelling offer. There are seven qualities of compelling offers:

1. **High perceived value:** Think a free gutter with a new roof or a free front door if you replace all your windows rather than a five percent discount.

2. **Very, very low friction:** Your offer has to be easy to claim.

3. **Urgency:** You need to incentivize people to take action. Give them a hard deadline (e.g., a seasonal deadline such as, "Do this now before winter!").

4. **Scarcity:** Make it a limited-time offer and a limited number of people who will receive it.

5. **Risk reversal:** Offer a guaranteed warranty with nothing to lose—anything that eliminates all of their objections.

6. **Payment options:** Make it easy for people who may not have the funds to take advantage of your offer with zero interest, no payments until next year, etc.

7. Strong call to action: Tell people exactly what you want them to do: Call now. Claim this offer. Speak to an expert.

The combination of a compelling offer and a landing page that guides a prospective customer to do exactly what you want them to do can make a huge difference in the results of your ad investment.

Work with a Lead-Generation Partner

Your lead-generation partner should provide you with a tracking number that allows you to see revenue per lead, otherwise you don't really know if you're making money with them. More importantly, you want to understand how much revenue is coming in per lead. You want to see customer acquisition marketing reports. Beware of vanity metrics like click-throughs. What you want to know is how many of their leads did you actually close? And what was the quality of those leads? Are you getting a bunch of $50 leads and fewer $300 leads? If your goal is $1,200, for example, you need 24 $50 leads vs. four $300 leads. It's better to pay more money for an amazing lead.

For more information about lead generation for your company, visit homeservicemillionaire.com/lead-gen.

Shows and Events

Home Shows

Another potential source of leads are home shows. I was talking with the owner of the largest window company on the West Coast at a home show recently. He was telling me how he cut out 90 percent of his advertising spend and shifted his focus to doing just one thing—and he doubled his business. Naturally, that got my attention.

"I used to be one of the largest TV and billboard ad spenders in the industry," he said, "but a friend of mine said I should check out home-show events because they're very profitable."

"OK," I said, "How profitable?"

"I spend about 10 percent of what I was spending before, and I have doubled my business. With the right training and the right team, you can get your advertising spend down as low as five percent of your revenue."

This sounded crazy to me at the time considering I was spending almost 20 percent of my revenue on advertising!

The cool thing about home-show events is they attract potential customers for you, all in one place, all for the price of the booth space. Home-show events are one of the best lead-generation machines out there!

I admit it is a lot of work to do a home-show event properly. But if you understand who your ideal customer is, what kind of events they go to, and how to approach them, and then take the time to hone your process, you will save a lot of time and money up front and get great results.

If you do shows, it's really important to get the right people to work at your booth. But where do you find them? You know those salespeople working the kiosks that are in the center aisle of the mall? The ones who will find a way to engage you even if you're trying not to make eye contact? Who can make you believe your credit cards aren't safe without their brushed-aluminum RFID protective wallet? Not only are those folks not afraid of rejection, they also know an opening when they see it and are compelled to close it—and they'll close your deals too.

Tip: Provide the people working at the show with an iPad that has your PDF brochure loaded into iBooks. Then they can offer to email visitors your literature and do it right while they're standing there, as well as ask if it's OK to add them to your mailing list. Even better, have ServiceTitan loaded up and your employee can set the appointment then and there!

Community Events

Prospective customers are all around you. Get involved in your local community. Sponsor a sports team. Go to your local networking events to make connections. Get a table at local shows.

A colleague of mine, Mark Montgomery, used to run a security door company. He did a lot of local shows, and he told me he used to get tons of leads by taking a table at the local high school football game and handing out cards and cups of Gatorade. This gave him the opportunity to talk to all the moms and dads there to see their kids play—his ideal customers!

Everything you have done up until this point has been about lead generation. Remember: You've got to measure the effectiveness of all of these different tactics so you can do more of what works and stop what doesn't.

Already have leads? Great. In the next chapter, I'll show you how to turn those leads into cash money through sales. ▶▶▶

CHAPTER 5

SALES SUPERSTAR

Turning Leads into Sales

The key to going from a single start-up $50,000 in debt to a multicompany enterprise with more than $30 million dollars a year in revenue?

Sales.

You have to get great at it.

Why? Because to achieve your goals, you need to be able to consistently go out to a home or business, talk to a customer, accurately identify their problems and opportunities, and get the job. If you don't get the job, you can't do the job, get paid, and leave your

SALES SUPERSTAR ■ 103

customer happy so they'll tell their friends and call you again in the future.

If you want to be a home service millionaire, you have to get great at sales, and that means doing what you need to do to start sweeping all that money you're leaving on the table into your pocket.

Here are some questions for you: Do you know exactly what your closing ratio is? How did you get that number? Let's say you know that number for sure. Is it great or just average? Are you satisfied with average? I'm not—and no home service millionaire I know would be either.

So what are you doing to improve that closing ratio? Even if you think it's already great, you should always be working to make it better because that's what millionaires do.

Getting the Appointment

Once your customer relationship management (CRM) system is in place, you can start using it to follow up with new and old leads. At A1 Garage Door Service, we do not quote over the phone unless we have all of your information. This is an example of how the conversation goes after we find out the customer wants a quote. (We always—*always*—try to get our salesperson to the home for a free estimate first.)

> **Mr. Smith:** "I would like a quote over the phone. I don't want to waste your time coming out here."
>
> **Customer Service Representative (CSR):** "Sure, Mr. Smith, can I ask you a question? Are you looking for a quality product that will last or just a contractor solution to get you by for a year or so?"
>
> **Mr. Smith:** "Well, I want affordable, but I also want it to last. Can I have a few options?"
>
> **CSR:** "Sure you can. If you are happy with one of my options, how soon can we do the work?" (This is super important because

we want to find out what process he is going through to pick the company he will go with.)

Mr. Smith: "If I like what you say, I'll have you come out and do the work."

CSR: "OK, no problem. I don't want to quote you something over the phone and not have it be accurate. Can I grab your email so I can send you the quote? That way you can take a look at it and be sure it is exactly what you want."

Mr. Smith: "Sure. Here it is!"

CSR: "OK, the way our customer service program works is I have to collect just a few more things in order to send a quote. All I need now is your first and last name, property address for service, and the best phone number for you. Then the system will allow me to send this right out to you."

Mr. Smith: "Sure, here you go."

CSR: "OK, I'm going to follow up shortly to see if this works for you."

Now I have all the information to follow up with the customer. I can go in and set up follow-up tasks in our system, and you can bet that most of the time we are able to close. I can guarantee most of your competitors do not have a system like this in place.

Tip: If you're looking for a way to track your customer calls to have complete insight into all of their interactions over the phone and you don't have ServiceTitan yet, check out homeservicemillionaire.com /call-tracking.

You can see why having rock-star CSRs answering the phone is so critical to your call booking rate. To give you even more insight into the importance of this role, I've asked Erica Leonor from Power Selling Pros to weigh in. Erica has trained hundreds of CSRs in the home service industry. Here's what she said.

ROCK-STAR CSRs

Erica Leonor, Power Selling Pros

It's all about the relationship now. Customers are no longer satisfied to just have you come out and fix something; they want to connect and have that interaction be memorable. That's right—your customers want an *experience* to go along with their service.

Answering your incoming phone calls and emails well is your first priority, because without that technicians go home early and sales consultants do not have appointments. If the customer does not like the first impression, they will go somewhere else.

That's why having rock-star CSRs is so important. A CSR is the customer's first contact with you. They set the stage for what to expect from everyone else they may interact with—from the dispatcher to the tech or sales consultant.

Gone are the days where people order something from a catalog and think it's OK to wait around for two weeks to get the product. Companies that are obsessed with customer service, such as Nordstrom, Chick-fil-A, Amazon, and others, have changed all that. As the owner, it's your responsibility to figure out how to meet these ever-growing expectations of a unique and pleasant buying experience at every juncture.

Here's a real example of how you can start out great and kill the customer experience at the end. (Company name has been redacted to protect the guilty.) My boss, Brigham, recently moved and called to get one of those portable storage containers dropped in his driveway. It was easy to set up the appointment, and the container was delivered exactly when the company said it would be. He loaded it up, and they picked it up on time. All good.

The trouble started when he called to get the container dropped off at the new location. On that call, the CSR said, "I'm sorry; we are backed up. We don't have anyone to bring the container out for two weeks. Yes, I'm sorry, you will have to pay for the extra days too."

There are so many things wrong with that interaction it's hard to know where to start. I can tell you that Brigham will never use that service again and will recommend to others that they avoid it!

We do business with people we like and who treat us well, so the question is, what can we do to optimize that customer contact to set the tech or sales consultant up for success? Answer: set expectations and then work hard to exceed them. Here's an example of what I mean.

Recently I needed to find a new dentist. I'm very picky about who works on my teeth, so I called around to about 12 different offices, unimpressed. Then I called an office whose receptionist sounded amazing over the phone, and I immediately booked the appointment. When I got to the office and checked in, I was presented with a goodie bag containing movie tickets and other swag! The first contact I had with that office set and then *exceeded* my expectations.

How to Create Rock-Star CSRs

A lot of owners think the key to hiring a great CSR is to hire a nice person. That is a good start, but if all you do with that nice person is quickly run them through your policies and processes, give them a script, and turn them loose to answer the phones, your customers will be disappointed. Why? Because their first experience with your company will be a series of robotic responses that focus on your policies and processes rather than on listening and building the relationship.

To overcome this problem, you need to look at who is leading that team. Ultimately, it has to be you. Hopefully you are already recording calls for training purposes. If you are, take some time to listen to those phone calls. What you hear may surprise you (and not necessarily in a good way).

Are your CSRs inspired to perform at the highest level? If they aren't, the first person you should look at is you. Because what we've learned is if they have been trained and still aren't performing, it is usually because there's something negative going on in the culture. In fact, at Power Selling Pros, one of the first things we work on is helping owners get the company culture, principles, and core values aligned. Everything starts there.

Don't Be Sorry

There are a few things you can ask your CSRs to change that will make a big difference in your calls immediately. It's about vocabulary, and it's super important.

Listen to those calls. If you hear your CSRs telling customers, "Unfortunately, we can't do that," that is a bad thing. When you first meet someone do you really want to hear, "No, we can't," much less "unfortunately?" I don't!

Another one is, "I'm sorry, but we . . ." The problem with that approach is you've just implied it is the customer's fault.

Compare "I'm sorry to keep you holding" to "Wow, thank you for holding." Which one makes you feel better?

Saying "I'm sorry" is even worse when it's used to respond to a customer who is telling you something personal, such as, "The air-conditioning is out and my mother-in-law can't tolerate the heat." "I'm sorry" in that situation is just lazy and disingenuous. Instead say, "Wow, that sounds terrible. Here's what we can do."

The key is to always focus on what you *can* do for the customer rather than what you *can't* do. This requires a vocabulary shift. Here's how it works.

SCENARIO 1

Mrs. Smith: "Can you give me a ballpark price on that?" (If you're like most home service businesses, your CSRs hear that question several times a day!)

CSR: "I'm sorry, we don't give prices over the phone."

Mrs. Smith: "I really need to know about how much this is going to cost before I book the appointment."

CSR: "I can send a tech out for a $98 diagnostic fee and he can tell you exactly what it will cost."

Mrs. Smith: "Let me think about it and I'll call you back if I am interested." (Never calls back.)

SCENARIO 2 (*BETTER*)

Mrs. Smith: "Can you give me a ballpark price on that?"

CSR: "I need a little more information. What's going on?" (This tells the customer they are being listened to. Customers want to be cared about and reassured. They want their emotional needs taken care of.)

Mrs. Smith: "Well, the furnace isn't working right and it's really cold in the house."

CSR: "That sounds terrible. How long has this been going on?"

Mrs. Smith: "It just started yesterday, and then the heat cut out. That's why I'm calling you."

CSR: "Here's what we can do. Let's send out a comfort advisor. He'll do a heat load calculation so we can dial in the right solution and give you an accurate price. When would you like us out there?"

Mrs. Smith: "Wait, I really want a ballpark price."

CSR: "If I give you a price over the phone and the comfort advisor comes out and tells you something different, you'll be mad at me. Let's have the comfort advisor come out so we get it right the first time for you."

Mrs. Smith: "OK."

Cancel the Word Cancellation

Let's say one of your techs finishes a job early, so you call the next customer on the schedule to move up the appointment.

CSR: "Mr. Smith, we had a cancellation. Let's move up your appointment."

Mr. Smith: "OK." (Thinks, "Why did those people cancel? What do they know that I don't?")

Instead you want to say, "Mr. Smith, we have an earlier opening at 2:30 p.m. Would you like us to come earlier?" or "Mr. Smith, we had a reschedule and could come at 2:30 p.m. Would that work for you?"

This way you can move the appointment without creating a negative impression or doubt in the customer's mind.

Empowering CSRs

Imagine how empowering it would be to give your CSRs tools to take someone who was a "no" at the beginning of a call and turn them into a "yes," to teach them how to customize every phone call so they become fundamentally great at creating likability.

Rock-star CSRs are a vital part of your business, with the ability to provide customers with early "wow" experiences and positive emotional impacts—experiences that can ensure a successful start to new relationships that great service and follow-ups will allow you to profit from for years to come.

Please visit homeservicemillionaire.com/rockstar-csr for more information.

Tommy's Eight-Step Sales Process

've hired and trained several hundred technicians who have made thousands of sales. Here are eight steps for making sales of home services that I've found work every time. Share these steps with your techs and watch what happens.

Contact

Be considerate and manage expectations. When setting the appointment, give the customer a four-hour window of time when you will show up. About 30 minutes before you are due to arrive, call the customer and start to build rapport.

Say, "Hi, Mrs. Smith, I'm going to be there in about 30 minutes, but don't worry if you have to run out and do an errand. I'll give you a call when I'm about five minutes away. And when I get done, your garage door is going to work better than it has ever worked before."

Remember, there's never a second chance to make a first impression. Take a look at yourself before you get out of the truck. Tuck your shirt in. If you smoke cigarettes or tend to work up a sweat on the job, make sure to carry breath spray and deodorant—and use them *before* you walk into the customer's house.

Arrival

Park in the street. You never want to block the owners from having full access to their own home. The one exception to this is if you are visiting a big house with a spacious driveway and plenty of room for people to get in and out.

Be confident! You are the expert. Take control of the situation and make the customer feel like they chose the right company. At the same time, be humble and avoid saying things that might make the customer feel dumb. You want to make them feel like a genius for hiring you.

The first few minutes of the customer experience are key. If it's a bad experience they may let you finish the job, but they may not refer you or call you back. Show good manners and stay humble. Make eye contact and project confidence.

Assessment

Ask good questions. After I introduce myself and hand the customer my business card—but before I open my toolbox—there are three questions I ask:

1. This is a beautiful home; how long have you lived here?
2. What exactly is going on with the garage door?
3. Is this the first time you have had an issue?

By asking how long they have lived at the home, I'm learning if they have lived there for a while and how long they plan on living there. It also tells me a lot of things about the door. There might be things that have happened in the past with it, or the customer may have just moved in and never thought about it until it broke.

The second question—"What exactly is going on with the door?"— is, of course, the most important. Sometimes they'll tell me what they think (e.g., "This thing's so noisy none of us can sleep when Mr. Smith comes home from work, and we've wanted to change this door out for a while"), when in fact it's just a garage door spring that is broken. I've also had customers tell me they need new rollers and bearing plates (and be right) before I had a chance to look for myself.

The third question—"Is this the first time you have had an issue?"—allows me to determine whether the customer has ever had work done on the door and, more importantly, whether someone from *my* company has been out to the house previously. If the customer says, "You guys were out here two months ago," I'm just going to fix it. If I told the customer, "Well, those are the wrong springs," when it was *my* company that installed them, 100 percent of my legitimacy goes out the window.

The best way to make a customer happy is to ask good questions and then do a lot of listening *before* you get started. This will also increase your chances of finding and solving all their problems in one visit. Win-win!

Pitch

Sell the minimum product or service first—don't oversell. I had a technician out recently about my pool heater, and instead of taking time to listen to me he started trying to sell me lights, different mobile switches, and all kinds of other stuff. I kicked him out!

That's called "overselling" and it's a big mistake. Customers need to be able to trust you know what you're talking about and are being honest about their situation before they will open their wallets for more.

When a technician takes his time and shows me exactly what I'm going to get, and it's exactly what I was looking for, I say yes because I trust him and his approach. Once I trust him, I'm going to pull out my credit card or checkbook and make a purchase—it's a done deal.

Always go in with the minimum viable solution for what the customer called you about. Once the work is started, you can and should look around for other things that may have gone wrong during a general inspection.

Checklist Inspection

You should have a checklist that details every single thing that should be looked at on a job so it's done the same way every time. There is also a record of the inspection in case anything should go wrong later. Go through each item on the checklist (parts, etc.) and pass or fail the item. Take pictures of everything. Explain that as the last professionals who have seen the door, water heater, or electrical panel, you must create a record of the current state of the system.

Compliment the customer on the things that passed, and then go over the failed items using as many senses as possible. Let the customer see and touch the failed part and explain its significance. Show them animations and pictures to convince them of its importance.

Then do "show and tell." On a garage door, that means taking the door apart so you can compare the broken part to the brand-new one. As much as you can, get the customer to touch, see, smell, or hear the difference between the two parts. I call this the five senses rule. Get the customer to see and touch as many broken or worn parts as possible, and use very positive terms when describing the new parts. Good examples would be "machine pressed," "lifetime quality," or "made in the United States."

Develop simple ways to describe the way parts work. For example, if a roller is not rolling and the circumference has worn down, I tell people it's like driving down the freeway with your emergency brakes on. It does not make sense because those rollers are made to roll, not skid along the rails like they are doing. Keep it simple!

Package Pricing

Start to package (or bundle) what the customer needs into a total price. If there are items that are vital to safe operations, explain that to the customer.

Provide the customer with a written copy of your quote with accurate and verifiable information about your service and its cost. Then, be willing to go through the quote with them line by line if necessary. Be humble! In other words, show your expertise, but do not make the customer feel stupid.

Make your presentation as visual as possible. For example, you could include manufacturer's cut sheets showing the equipment and its features and benefits or before-and-after photos of previous jobs.

Why? Because only 10 percent of people remember what they hear, but 80 percent of people remember what they see up to three days after seeing it. (If you own a garage door or window company, check out homeservicemillionaire.com/simulator. This tool allowed us to literally triple our closing rates.)

Then, ask questions that will allow you to verify that the prospective customer understands and agrees with your proposal.

This is especially important when selling to the elderly. Be patient and prepared to offer extra reassurance and explain things more than once if needed.

People also love having price options: high, middle, and cheap. Limit options to three, because too many options can work against you. Always start with the best option and step down from there. Make sure that the middle option is profitable for you, because that's what most people will choose. The cheap option will allow you to compete on price, even though that's not your priority.

I always explain to the customer that the bottom package is there to match our competition, and that it's a builder-grade product with an almost nonexistent warranty. Then, I use positive adjectives to describe the better packages (e.g., "rollers" vs. "machine-pressed internal, self-lubrication, high-cycle rollers"). You would be surprised what a good adjective can do for a sale.

Backup

Dr. Robert Cialdini has studied the way sales are made for more than three decades. In his book *Influence: Science and Practice*, he said it's very hard for people to say "no" twice in a row. If you find it hard to close a sale, or a customer seems upset, get your manager on the phone.

Calling up a manager while making a sale is *not* calling a fake person and acting like you're giving a discount! Call the actual manager (who optimally knows you're out on a sales call) and put them on the phone so they can make sure the customer understands exactly *why* they need to do what you say is necessary. When I'm in that manager role what I usually do is ask the technician exactly what he went over with the customer, and then ask the customer what else they need— bottom rubber, rollers, or a keypad?

If you have to discount the price to get the job, try to get something in return—a positive review on Yelp, a referral, or permission to leave a sign in their front yard. I've even had a happy customer set up a meeting with the president of their homeowner's association in response to a discounted price. What I have found is that most customers just want a so-called good deal. Usually, I'm able to up the sale and give them something extra that doesn't cost a whole lot.

When you talk to a customer, your vocabulary should exactly match that of your customer. This should apply to your technicians as well. Be polite but firm in your voice and behavior.

If you incorporate these tactics effectively, you could turn your 70 percent closing rate into a 90 percent closing rate very quickly.

Close the Sale

What is the last thing you tell a customer before walking out of their home? I probably say this line 10 times a day: "Sir/Ma'am, what is it going to take to earn your business today? The reason I ask is we have grown our business more than 40 percent because of referrals, and once we do this service for you, I am sure you are going to tell your friends, neighbors, and family all about us."

Now *shut up*.

Listen carefully and find out exactly what the buying criteria is for the customer.

If you have to ask an uncomfortable sales question, ask it with confidence and then shut up. Wait for the answer, even if it means that seconds tick by in empty silence. Don't jump in and start qualifying your question before the person has given an answer.

When you've assessed the broken garage door and you've said something like, "We can have this door operating like new for $500," say nothing else until the customer responds. Your attitude must be, "We want to serve you, but we're not desperate. The choice is yours."

Finally, if you're having trouble closing the sale, remember to call your manager for backup! If you have closed the sale, the next step is to secure the relationship.

Secure the Relationship: You've packed up your tools and made sure the site is perfectly clean. You've filled out all the paperwork, collected payment, and explained the warranties. Are you done? Not quite.

Stop and invest a few moments in securing your new customer relationship. Take a little time to describe everything you have done. The goal is to make them think, "Wow, that sure was worth the money."

For example, if you do garage doors, you should run the door five or six times and show them how you cleaned the work area and left no grease anywhere. Explain how the safety features work. Show that you care about the customer's experience and want to make sure everything was pleasant. Hand them a business card and say, "If you have any problems, please call me on my cell phone and I will get right back out here."

Taking time with the customer at the job's end eliminates buyer's remorse and prevents warranty callbacks. It also increases the chances of a good review and reduces the likelihood of a bad one should something go awry after you leave.

Responding to Customer Objections

If you went to the doctor, and she said, "I'm going to prescribe a medicine for you—take two pills twice a day," how would you respond?

You'd probably say, "Before I take it, I have some questions. What are the side effects? Will it make me sleepy? Can I get a cheaper generic version? How long will I have to take it?" And so on.

Your doctor would then (hopefully) patiently answer your questions and explain the benefits of your medication. *Then* you'd go home and start taking it.

You are now comfortable with the idea of taking the medicine and are willing to own it.

Home services are no different. Whether you're selling HVAC units, solar panels, new bathrooms, hot water heaters, or, like me, garage doors, you're going to encounter customers who need to get comfortable with you and your service before they are willing to own it.

Sales trainers call those tough questions customers ask sales objections. The primary rule of overcoming objections is that you need to find those areas where you and the homeowner can agree. Following are the five most common objections I hear and some scripts you can use to guide your responses. Share with your techs and start closing those sales!

"I Need to Talk to My Significant Other."

This one is usually a smoke screen or a white lie. The first thing you need to do is determine what is really at issue. Your goal is to get to the truth so you can overcome the *real* objection.

> **Mrs. Smith:** "I need to discuss this with my partner. We like to make monetary decisions together."
>
> **Technician:** "That is exactly what I would do too. Do you think

he will have some questions or concerns about what we have discussed today?"

Mrs. Smith: "Yes, knowing him, he will want to know all the information."

Technician: "No problem, do you have an idea of what kind of questions he will ask?"

Mrs. Smith: "Most likely about the pricing."

Technician: "I can provide you with that information, no problem. Will he have questions on the technical part of the installation process?"

Mrs. Smith: "I think his main concern will be pricing."

Technician: "I see the concern. What do you predict he will say about pricing?"

Mrs. Smith: "That the price is too high."

Technician: "What are your thoughts on the price?" (Listens while the customer voices her concerns.) "Let's make sure both you and your partner understand the full picture. I've gathered a lot of information today, and I know you need to review it together as well. May I return later this afternoon and review it with you both? Five o'clock is open for me. Does that work for you?"

"It's Too Expensive."

You've completed your presentation and established the value of your services, so you're ready to address any objections. The goal here is to build upon the customer's needs and wants.

What you need to understand is when a customer first hears your price—especially if you're not undercharging—it can be a shock to their system. Everyone reacts to this type of shock differently. Some customers get pretty defensive and others get downright rude! This is where it becomes really important for you to remain in control of *your* emotions. You've spent time building rapport with this customer, and unless you know how to properly diffuse their reaction you may never get them to say yes.

Mrs. Smith: "The price you quoted is too high."

Technician: "Mrs. Smith, I understand what a surprise this investment can be, especially when you weren't thinking that these repairs would be needed. I just want to confirm I have answered all your questions and addressed all your concerns. Would you say the repairs I've shown and outlined here are things your home is in need of?"

Mrs. Smith: "I do agree all these repairs are needed for my home, but the cost to do them is just too expensive."

Technician: "Definitely understandable, Mrs. Smith. If I can just clarify—when you say 'too expensive,' is it too expensive to fit into your budget? Or is it that you don't feel it's a reasonable amount for the services I will be providing?"

Mrs. Smith: "There's no way the services you quoted are worth the price you are asking."

Technician: (Feels angry, but remembers to stay in control of his emotions.) "Mrs. Smith, I would like to apologize for our price. I am aware that we charge more than other companies. But here's the thing. I'd rather apologize one time for the price I quoted being too high than apologize multiple times for poor service. Would you like to know why?"

Mrs. Smith: "Yes."

Technician: "I've found that three things in this business are true. Would you like to know what they are?"

Mrs. Smith: "Sure."

Technician: "As a customer you have three basic rights: you have the right to the lowest price, first and foremost; you have the right to a great, reputable, and highly trained technician; and you have the right to an amazing company that stands behind all its work, keeps its promises, and continues to give great service even after the job has been completed. Would you agree these are your rights as a customer?"

Mrs. Smith: "Absolutely."

Technician: "Great. So, here's the thing—you can have a great technician and the lowest price, or you can have a company with an OK reputation and the lowest price. But if it's quality work, outstanding service, and guarantees in writing you're after, this is actually an amazing price. Wouldn't you say the knowledge that you have a great company behind you, who has your best interests in mind from the start, is worth a little more?"

Mrs. Smith: "Having it explained that way makes sense."

"I Simply Can't Afford That."

If the customer understands the value but says they can't afford it, what they may actually be saying is, "I can't afford it right now" or "I can't afford to pay for it all at once." In either case, you can assist the customer in their buying decision by finding out if the customer would be interested in financing, alternative buying options, or service agreements.

Technician: "I know the need for this investment was a bit of a surprise, Mrs. Smith, because you had no idea you needed a new opener. I just want to make sure that I have answered all your questions and addressed all your concerns. Do you agree the new opener I recommended is what your garage needs?"

Mrs. Smith: "I do. I just didn't expect it to be that much."

Technician: "I completely understand, Mrs. Smith."

Financing: At this point, you have three closing options. The first is financing.

> **Technician:** "Mrs. Smith, you have expressed your concern with affordability on this investment. There are options that would make this process very simple for you. I would like to offer you a solution that would allow you to get everything you wanted and at the same time make it affordable. How does that sound?"
>
> **Mrs. Smith:** "Yes, of course, that would be very helpful."
>
> **Technician:** "That's great news! So, Mrs. Smith, we do have a couple of great finance options that would bring your total cost to $37 a month. If this is still a little high for your budget, we could evenly distribute the payments out as far as five years. So that would drop your monthly cost even more to $20. So, if this sounds like something you would like to proceed with, we can get started with the safety of your door today."
>
> **Mrs. Smith:** "Yes, I like the sound of that."

Alternative Buying Options: There will be times where financing is not the answer or even an option for some customers. In that case, what you want to do is provide the customer with some additional buying options.

> **Technician:** "Mrs. Smith, the most important thing is that your problem is resolved." (Go back over the reason why she called you out.) "However, after doing the full inspection, I came across some other safety concerns. The ultimate goal is to make sure the door is safe and the repairs are within your budget. We can go through the list and identify the

most important issues that are outside of the main problem if you'd like."

Mrs. Smith: "That sounds great." (Tech goes through the list.) "I feel X, Y, and Z should be addressed today, and A, B, and C can wait."

Technician: "OK, just to clarify, you would like to do X, Y, and Z today, Mrs. Smith?"

Mrs. Smith: "Yes, I would like those done today."

Service Agreements: The last closing option is to focus on the benefits of your service and service agreements. I will talk more about service agreements later in this chapter, when we talk about how to keep existing customers engaged.

Technician: "I know this is more than you were anticipating paying, Mrs. Smith, and my priority, besides safety, is that you feel confident in the options you have. For example, did you know we have a service agreement available that would ensure you get all the repairs on your list at the best possible price?"

Mrs. Smith: "I did not know that. How does that work?"

Technician: "OK, so let me go over everything with you, Mrs. Smith. If you add a service agreement, you can see how the 15 percent discount takes your total bill down to $997. Adding the service agreement is a great way to get the best of both worlds because the annual cost is only $47. You will definitely get back 100 percent of that investment just in preventative services and client specials. Would you like to move forward with the service agreement along with the other things on the list?"

Mrs. Smith: "Sure, let's do that."

"I Need Two Additional Bids."

Another objection you may run into is the customer wanting to get additional bids before they make their decision.

Mrs. Smith: "So I just wanted to let you know that I need to get three bids before I can make my decision."

Technician: "That is understandable. If you don't mind me asking, what criteria will you be using to make a decision?"

Mrs. Smith: "Of course, the lowest price will be the deciding factor."

Technician: "OK, that is ideal, but besides the price, are there any other factors that would help determine your choice? For example, service, follow through, quality of the job, or warranties and guarantees both in writing and verbal?"

Mrs. Smith: "Oh yes, all those things are important." (Your goal now is to shift to helping Mrs. Smith make the value the priority.)

Technician: "So price, service, follow through, job quality, and warranties and guarantees are all important factors in making your decision. Got it. As far as price goes, when most homeowners want the lowest price they never anticipate that it may come with a bad installation. Would you agree with that, Mrs. Smith?"

Mrs. Smith: "That's true."

Technician: "Most homeowners like yourself want the best value for their money. Would you agree that you want the best value?"

Mrs. Smith: "Yes, when you put like that, that is what I am saying."

Technician: "Mrs. Smith, I realize you can get this work done cheaper elsewhere. And while I can't speak to the quality of other technicians or companies, I feel confident enough to stand behind the work we do. We use only premium-quality parts, and we make sure to fix the problem properly instead of doing a quick fix or taking a shortcut that may lead to a worse situation later. So while you may get a cheaper price somewhere else, I don't believe you will get the job done better than we do it or get a better value than what my company can offer. Isn't that what you are looking for? The best value?"

Mrs. Smith: "Yes, that's what I'm looking for."

Technician: "So, Mrs. Smith, if you feel the same as I do, would you also agree I have proven my quality of work in a professional manner as well as provided a written guarantee that I am the best value?"

Mrs. Smith: "OK, I have made my decision. I will go with your company."

"I Need Some Time to Think about It."

If your customer is not ready to make a buying decision, empathy is important. Keep in mind that customers may become defensive or guarded. What you say or do next is critical to making sure this technique works.

Mrs. Smith: "I need some time to think about it."

Technician: "That is understandable, Mrs. Smith. This is an important decision, and I know you wouldn't waste your time thinking about something if you were not seriously considering or interested in it, right?"

Mrs. Smith: "That is correct. I am interested. I just want to think about this decision."

Technician: "And so we are both on the same page, you do feel that the options I provided are what your home is in need of, correct?"

Mrs. Smith: "Yes, and you have proven that to me."

Technician: "That's good to hear, because I got a little worried I might have ruffled your feathers a bit and you wanted to politely ask me to leave. That's not the case here, is it, Mrs. Smith?" (The customer may appear shocked or surprised following this question.)

Mrs. Smith: "No, not at all. I feel you are a great technician and just doing your job."

Technician: "Thank goodness. The last thing I wanted to do was offend my customer." (By using the present tense you assume she is already your customer.)

Technician: "To make sure we're clear as you are thinking through your decision, I just have a few more questions. Were all the options I gave you the problem? Do you think it is the quality of my work that would concern you? Would you say it is the reputation of my company that's in question? Do you have any questions about our warranties or guarantees?" (Assuming the answer to all of these questions is "No," go over the proposal and reconfirm any other value points you offer.) "OK, so now that we have those questions out of the way, Mrs. Smith, can you level with me? Is it the investment that is the cause of your concern?"

Mrs. Smith: "Honestly, that is the biggest part of it. This is just a lot of money for me."

Technician: "I understand where you are coming from. Would it be OK to ask you another question?"

Mrs. Smith: "Yes, no problem."

Technician: "In your head you most likely had a number that it was roughly going to be, correct?"

Mrs. Smith: "Yes, that is true."

Technician: "That is common. Most people do. And if that number was the same number on this page, chances of you filling out paperwork right now would be pretty high, wouldn't you say?"

Mrs. Smith: "Yes."

Technician: "OK, can you let me know how much is too much?"

Mrs. Smith: "Yes, the amount is $200 more than I was anticipating."

This is where you revert back to the three closing options—financing, alternative buying options, or service agreements—and close the sale based off the information you gather.

Financing is a great way to allow your customers to purchase the products and services they really want and need, which results in higher ticket totals for you. To explain how financing works, I asked the finance master—Darius Lyvers, chief operating officer of Fairfax, Virginia-based HVAC and electrical company F. H. Furr—to weigh in.

THE RIGHT WAY TO INTRODUCE FINANCING

Darius Lyvers, COO, F. H. Furr

To make any sale, a customer must be both willing and able to buy. If you can eliminate *able*, then all you need to work on is the customer's willingness. The best way to make customers able to purchase is to offer financing.

Consider the typical sit-down with a customer, which goes something like this: "Mrs. Smith, we can take care of your immediate problem and change the blower motor, and the charge for that is $1,023. We can take care of the blower motor and address the humidification issues, and that will be $2,063. And if you want to add the filtration system we can do that and clean out your ducts, too, for a total of $4,533."

The problem is, when the customer booked the appointment, they were expecting to spend *hundreds* of dollars, not thousands!

As soon as the technician said the first number—$1,023—Mrs. Smith didn't hear a thing he had to say about options two and three. She was just trying to come to terms with the fact that this repair was not going to be a few hundred bucks. As soon she heard the number $1,023, she checked out.

Let's revisit the same conversation, this time using financing options: "Mrs. Smith, we can take care of the immediate problem and change the blower motor, and the charge for that is $7 a month. We can take care of the blower motor and install the humidification system for $18 a month. And we can do all of that plus take care of the filtration system and the duct cleaning for another $13 or $14 a month."

Right there, the tech has made it possible for the customer to afford every single option he has offered.

Mrs. Smith was able to listen and think, "I can afford that. I can afford that. I can afford that." By providing her with financing options, the tech is ensuring Mrs. Smith is *able* to buy all the recommendations, whereas without financing, she may not have been able to buy anything at all.

The Answer to "Do You Need Financing?" Is Always "No"

One of the biggest mistakes people make is asking the question, "Do you need financing?" The technician will hear "no" far more than "yes" and eventually stop offering financing altogether. The answer is always no, and here are five reasons why:

1. Pride: In this case, the customer is insulted. They are thinking, "Does it look like I need financing?"

2. Cash is king: This customer believes, "If I pay cash I may pay less."

3. Conditioned response: This customer fears that if they say "yes," they may buy something they don't want or need. Just saying "no" is a defense mechanism to help avoid buyer's remorse.

4. Previous experience: This customer may have endured a long, drawn-out process while applying for financing in the past, or maybe they were declined for a loan a few years ago.

5. It's expensive: This customer may relate financing

to interest and fees. There are many ways to leverage financing to save money, but the customer may not know their options yet.

The solution to this problem is *do not ask that question*!

Instead, format your presentation in a way that allows you to talk about financing in terms of a monthly payment. Assume the customer is going to want to finance because when she hears the different options, she may well say yes.

After hearing your presentation, the customer may say, "What's the total?" You can now show it because you've already introduced the low-payments option and made it affordable.

Everyone is a finance buyer. That said, there are three types of finance buyers—low interest, no interest, and low payments. Your tech can identify which type of buyer they are dealing with by simply *listening* to the customer's responses when presented with payment options:

1. Low-interest buyers: These buyers either don't have the money to pay for it up front or, if they do have the money, they want to keep it in reserve. They are willing to borrow money at a "reasonable" interest rate. You will hear questions like, "Is this your lowest interest rate?"

2. No-interest buyers: Some no-interest buyers have the money but want to leverage other people's money. Others are expecting a big influx of cash later (a commission, bonus, tax refund, etc.), which would allow them to pay off the purchase. They go with no interest because they expect things to get better. You will hear questions like, "Do you have anything with no interest?" or "Is this same-as-cash?"

3. Low-payments buyers: These are the people who are stretching it thin, and they just need the lowest payments possible stretched out for as long as possible. They need something that will meet their monthly budget. You will hear questions like, "Do you have anything with a lower payment?" or "Does that payment include everything?"

All your tech needs to do is listen. The customer will tell you what type of finance buyer they are!

Why Techs Don't Offer Financing to Your Customers

Most technicians aren't comfortable with offering financing, even though it would be tremendously beneficial to them and you. Here is why:

1. They sell like they buy: The tech thinks, "If they needed financing, they would ask for it." Or, "It's only $800. They don't need financing." Or, "They have a nice house and car, they can afford it."

The problem is they are selling out of their own pockets. Your number one challenge is to get them to realize their customers are *not* them. Train them to realize that how a customer pays is up to the customer to decide. We just provide the customer with all available options.

As a leader in your organization, it's up to you to change the mindset of your technicians. Train and role-play again and again in every meeting until talking about financing becomes second nature.

2. Change: Techs get into a rut when it comes to selling, and it's hard to get them to change their process. The first step is to approach the techs you know would be most open to change and turn them into financing ambassadors. When other techs see their colleagues start closing those $3,000, $4,000, or $5,000 tickets, they will see the light. Work with the techs you can change the fastest first. Then, watch as the program takes off. Often these "ambassadors" are the technicians who adopt new products or services with ease, look for opportunities (besides the reason they are at the call), and are not afraid of price.

3. It's complicated: There are a lot of steps to financing— applications, signatures, and deposits. Without automation, it's a lot of paper shuffling and a lot of math. No wonder your techs don't want to do it. If your company currently operates on a system that integrates financing, great! If not, keep it simple. Limit the number of steps needed to process the financing and, if you can, eliminate paperwork and calculations.

4. A confused mind says no: If you have too many financing options or the way those options work is confusing, the techs won't offer them. To overcome this problem, simplify your financing options as much as possible. Choose two or three plans to offer and provide the tech a handout with a few words to describe each plan. Making it as simple as possible for the technician to present financing options is the key to success.

Grow Your Business

Every customer is a potential finance buyer. Our job is to provide them with options. The customer's job is to decide what's best for them. Always assume financing and deliver with payments. Solve the "able" and both your conversion and average tickets will soar. Best of all, you are providing all your customers with the opportunity to take advantage of your services. If you are already delivering on payments and offering financing, do more of it. If you haven't started, hopefully you are my competitor, and I encourage you to keep doing what you are doing!

Learn more about financing at homeservicemillionaire.com /financing.

Safety First

What if you come across a dangerous situation but the customer refuses to have you fix the problem?

Safety—yours and the customer's—has to come first in any home service repair or installation. Not only could a customer be badly hurt, the lawsuit that may follow can also be devastating to a business. The example I use is it's like being a bartender. If you overserve a customer and they get hurt or hurt someone else, you're the one who gets in trouble. (That said, you do have liability insurance in case something bad happens, right? Right? Good.)

To be as safe as possible using the products you install and your service, you must document your offer of the exact safety feature you are offering and why. And if the customer refuses it, you must get documentation of exactly what you offered and then get them to sign off on it. If you do things over email, you still have to have a way to confirm the customer received that communication, preferably via a proposal that requires a signature. You can also opt to walk away from the job. And if you do that, document that you did so and why.

At A1 Garage we run into a lot of old doors that really shouldn't be repaired. As much as your customer may want you to repair it, remember you will have to defend your decision to go along with it if the product later fails. If warning labels are required, use them. If the customer doesn't want the label placed, have them sign on the work order that the label was refused. If you do place it, take a picture of it so you have proof it existed when you left the job.

Don't assume the customer can't afford a vital safety component. Always offer it and explain to the customer why they should let you install it. If the customer refuses the component, make sure they sign a statement documenting that you made them aware of the safety issue and they refused.

Dealing with Irate Customers

Every once in a while, you or your technician will have to deal with a customer who is angry about something. It may be that he thinks the previous technician did a lousy job, the garage door is defective, or you didn't get there fast enough.

Here's how to diffuse an angry customer and even turn them into a fan:

1. **Be calm and polite:** When the person you're talking to is tense, it's imperative that you keep cool and calm from beginning to end.

2. **Acknowledge their pain:** Show empathy by saying, "I'm sorry you are having these issues with your garage door. I'm here to help you."

3. **Let them vent:** The irate customer might go off on you and say something like, "This is all your fault! Your lousy company can't seem to fix anything! This is the third time you've been out here, and I still have this same problem." It's OK. Don't take it personally. Keep being nice. This is the time for the client to vent, not you.

   Once you feel you have your customer's attention, use the information from your observations to build what persuasion, compliance, and negotiation expert Dr. Robert Cialdini refers to as "connecting points."

   Let's assume you've already looked around. You noticed the electrical box in the garage was corroded and suspect the garage door motor isn't getting consistent power. You might say, "Sir, I noticed you have a corroded electrical box in the garage. Is it possible the garage door motor is not getting consistent power, which would make it work intermittently?" Show the customer the old circuit box. Chances are they'll say something like, "I saw that and was thinking about calling an electrician."

4. **Focus on creating solutions:** Having endured the customer's tirade, it would be easy to rub this obvious defect in his face. That would also be a mistake—if your company was involved with the garage door previously, your technician may have missed this problem too. What your customer needs is a *solution*, not excuses or explanations. You can be right but still not win! Being right is all some technicians care about. They need to understand *winning* is what really matters.

   Gently educate the customer. Apologize for not noticing the underlying problem and suggest a solution. If the problem *was* caused by a technician from your company, apologize profusely. If you're a company owner, your service technicians must have the confidence and ability to call you and get an immediate decision on whether to offer the irate customer a special deal or free service. Nothing makes a wronged customer happier faster than to have the problem fixed at no charge!

5. **Always look toward the future:** When you start any service call, it should be with the future in mind. You should ask yourself, "What will it take for this customer to be loyal and stay with us?" Most people are ready to forgive and forget, but only as long as they're treated with respect and courtesy and their problems are solved quickly.

Keeping Existing Customers

All home service providers need a way to keep customers engaged in between service calls because it's much easier and less expensive to keep selling to an existing customer than it is to acquire a new one. According to Brian Kaskavalciyan, president of gFour Marketing Group, it's vitally important to build a fence around your customers and take care of those existing relationships instead of continually chasing after new customers. In the next section, Brian shares his secrets for creating amazing customer retention.

BUILDING A FENCE AROUND YOUR CLIENTS

Brian Kaskavalciyan, President,
gFour Marketing Group

Your most profitable assets are your current and former clients. Yet most business owners are so busy chasing after the next new customer that they neglect the ones they already have!

To increase your business's profits, make it immune to competition, and ensure it is a valuable, sustainable asset you can rely on, you must have a system in place that maximizes the profit potential of every new client you acquire.

You may wonder why I say "client" instead of "customer." It is because the word "customer" implies someone who buys from you just once, while the word "client" implies a long-term relationship. Clients are people you care about, and who regard you as a partner in solving their problems and needs.

Without a strong, solid "fence" around your clients, chances are good they will wander away from you and onto your competitor's property. By "fence" I mean the constant nurturing and protection of that relationship, which is the only way you will ever achieve maximum profitability from it. Here's how it works.

Collect Prospect and Client Data

Your client base is a gold mine—more valuable than your offices, your warehouses, and even your top salespeople. To make the most of that rich resource, you need to be collecting as much information as possible on each client that walks through your door or calls your business. Begin with that information, and then work on cleaning up your existing client list and getting it into a CRM system.

Customers can be reluctant to share their information, so be prepared to bribe your clients to give it to you. Yes, bribe. For example, offer them a free system inspection, a coupon for a discount on future service, or additional system upgrades in exchange for their information. Then, make sure that information is immediately entered into your CRM system.

One way or another you have already paid to get that client to call you. Don't let them hang up without capturing their information.

Acknowledge and Appreciate

Taking the time to say thank you is one way of letting clients know they mean more to you than just another dollar. However, it's really important to say thank you in the right way. Here's how you can do just that.

Within 24 hours, have someone in your office make a phone call (we call it a "happy call") to make sure your client is satisfied and there aren't any issues. For example, you could say, "Hi Mrs. Smith, welcome to the A1 Garage family. I'm calling to thank you again for your business and make sure you're happy with the service we provided. Was the job done to your satisfaction? Was the technician professional?"

If they are happy, then you can ask, "Would you refer your friends and family to our business?"

Next, the owner should write the client an email, again thanking them for their business and making sure they are happy. This should happen within two days of the service call or product purchase. Here is a sample email:

Hi Mrs. Smith,

Just a note to thank you again for your business. We really appreciate it. If you are not absolutely thrilled with the service we provided I want to hear about it and we'll make it right. Here is my cell phone number and email address. Please feel free to call anytime.

Thank you,
Tommy Mello

The next day, a gift should arrive at your client's doorstep. Depending on what tier buyer they are, this gift can range from something as simple as a handwritten thank-you note to a box with a thank-you note and a jar of cookies branded with your logo. Here's an example of what to write in the thank-you note:

Dear Mrs. Smith,

Thank you so much for your business. I appreciate your choosing A1 Garage and I look forward to serving you again in the near future. If you need anything, please don't hesitate to call me. I'll be happy to help.

Again, thank you,
Tommy Mello

Last, within 10 to 30 days after the sale, send a letter from the owner, once again thanking the client for their recent business. Include a special offer for their next purchase (e.g., a gift, dollars-off coupon, or add-on service at no additional charge) and a referral request form. Prepare the letter ahead of time, postdate it, and put it into a tickler file to be mailed on the appropriate date.

Here's the thing—your goal is not just to stand out from your competition. It's to stand out from everybody they've ever done business with in the past. By taking this extra step for your clients, you automatically erase any potential feelings of buyer's remorse. You'll also reduce the number of refunds, bad reviews, and other consequences of unsurfaced client dissatisfaction, and develop a closer relationship with your clients and satisfy their desire to be acknowledged. They will see you as someone who can solve their problems and feel good about their experience with you and your company.

But that's not all. Not only will this process make the client more receptive to your next offer, you'll also be able to more easily solicit referrals and testimonials.

You may think your clients don't want to be bothered by communication from your company. This is not true. If people don't want to be bothered, they will tell you, and you can take them off the list. Our observation is that it's actually the owner who doesn't want to be bothered! Don't be that owner.

There's one final step in the "fencing-in" process.

Communicate (Keep in Touch)

A few years ago, we had a bug problem at one of my offices. We found a local pest control company, which came out and did a good job. The company billed us, we paid, and the transaction was complete. We were satisfied, and the pest control business owner must have been too because he got paid and received validation his ads were working.

A week went by. No communication from the pest control company. A month went by. Nothing. A few months later, we needed pest control again. Did we dig through our paperwork to see which company we used last time? No! We went back to Google and searched again. Did we use the same company? I have no idea.

The point is, the first pest control company made no attempt to profit from us a second, third, or even fourth time. And so that profit very likely went to someone else.

That's what I mean about building a fence around your clients. If you don't wrap them up in a relationship, they will wander off and the recurring profit you could have made will wander with them—right into your competitor's wallet.

For more information about how to increase your profits by focusing on retaining the clients you already have, visit homeservicemillionaire.com/customer-retention.

Email Marketing

Well-executed email marketing can help you stay top of mind in case your customers (or their neighbors) need your services. You should be collecting email addresses from every customer so you have the ability to keep in touch with them and offer helpful information and exclusive discounts.

But what do you put in those emails so your customers will actually look forward to reading them? The key to writing emails that the customer will enjoy reading and thus buying from you is to provide *value*. You can send them an email on their birthday or a monthly newsletter with home tips and coupons they can either use or pass on to a neighbor.

Remember, quality is better than quantity. You're better off having a smaller, highly responsive list than a huge list where no one ever emails you back or engages with your offers. Don't obsess over open rates. Focus on whether your emails are actually leading to sales!

Email marketing can be very effective, but it's a deep subject and we've just scratched the surface. To cut the learning curve and increase your chances of success out of the block, I recommend you partner with a professional copywriter who knows these principles. It will dramatically increase your chances of success.

Service Agreements

Residential and commercial service agreements—also called maintenance agreements, preventative maintenance contracts, and service contracts—typically include periodic maintenance, inspection, cleaning, and testing of equipment and accessories. They may also include additional customer benefits, such as discounts for repairs, overtime work at regular rates, or priority customer status.

How do service contracts benefit you, the business owner? Simple: they represent a storehouse of future service calls, booked in advance.

If your company has, say, 30 percent of its annual call volume already booked, then growth becomes easier. My observation is companies that complain about low call volume also typically have low service agreement numbers. Getting those service agreements signed is like putting money in the bank.

To gain more insights into how to be successful with service agreements, I reached out to Jaime DiDomenico, chief executive officer of CoolToday. Jaime has more than 14,000 (and counting) unique service agreement clients.

BUILDING RELATIONSHIPS WITH SERVICE AGREEMENTS

Jaime DiDomenico, CEO, CoolToday

The first thing to realize is that regardless of the service you provide, you are really in the *relationship* business. Realizing this one thing gives you a big advantage because most home service businesses are still transactional, meaning they come out, do the service call, and that is the last time the customer ever has any contact with them unless there's another problem.

There are a lot of myths around service and maintenance plans. Owners believe they are a loss leader or they can't be sold in the plumbing or electrical industry. They also believe service agreements are some kind of discount club for loyal customers, or that they will have to raise their prices to cover the benefits offered.

All of these ideas are totally false and here's why: the value is in the customer. When we analyzed three years of repairs and project invoices, we projected that over a 10-year period a transactional customer will spend an average of $667 while a relationship customer (defined as a customer who has maintained an agreement with us for more than two years) will spend $1,544!

Seven Steps to Building a Successful Service Agreement Program

1. Owners and general managers must believe: It all starts with you. Talk to your managers about the value of these agreements and get them to have these discussions with your staff in their weekly field or office meetings. Create a trifold brochure that techs can take to the job and leave with the customer.

2. There must be a champion: Appoint someone who is in charge of the agreement process and whose job it is to measure and report on the results.

3. Assign a good commission/spiff plan: This should include renewals made in the field and in the office. If your CSR gets a customer to renew the agreement, they should receive the same reward as the tech for their efforts.

4. There must be measurement: You want to know how many agreements are active, sold daily, how many have been sold by whom, etc. You also want to know the renewal rate. Share these results with your team. Make it a goal to convert 30 to 50 percent of those opportunities. (Note: This is easier to do if you have an integrated CRM system in place, such as ServiceTitan, which will provide you with ready access to those numbers.)

5. There must be high value to the customer for a low cost: Example offers include: four-hour service on our Total Today Care plan; waived diagnostic/trip charges with repair; 20 percent discount on repairs (all trades), except on equipment; free Freon with repair (up to two pounds), a $188 value; free basic toilet rebuild on plumbing plans, a $194 value; free camera inspection, a $93 value; or one free drain clearing annually, a $99 value.

6. Make the membership setup process as simple and flexible as possible: If you're still doing it manually, that means creating marketing and support collateral as well as documenting the process the tech needs to follow to be successful. (Note: ServiceTitan is developing an intuitive and flexible selling and setup wizard that allows memberships to have multiple duration and billing type options and allows you to create an equipment-based membership. It will also allow for customization at the point of sale.)

7. The culture has to treat these customers like gold: Hold people accountable for treating the relationships with customers like the gold they truly are!

What Agreements Could Mean for Your Company

Agreements reduce marketing expenses because you don't have to find as many new customers each month. They also drive up customer referrals. We've found our agreement customers are three times more likely to refer us to others. Agreements also allow you to better weather slow times because you always have a stream of income coming in from renewals.

The best thing about agreements, however, is that they allow you to grow a repeatable, renewable business, which increases the value of your business overall.

For more information on service agreements, visit home servicemillionaire.com/service-agreements.

The last two chapters have covered lead generation, paid online advertising, social media, sales techniques, customer relationship management, customer retention strategies, and more. But don't worry. You don't need to tackle everything at one time. Just pick a few things, focus, and get started.

In the next chapter, Performance Powerhouse, we'll talk about how to hire and energize the superstars you need to make all of this happen. ▶▶▶

CHAPTER 6

PERFORMANCE POWERHOUSE

Hire Superstars

S teve Jobs once said, "I noticed that the dynamic range between what an average person could accomplish and what the best person could accomplish was 50 or 100 to 1. Given that, you're well advised to go after the cream of the cream . . . A small team of A+ players can run circles around a giant team of B and C players." What it would mean to your business to have superstars in every position? Less stress? More business? Higher ticket averages? Lower turnover? I'll tell you what it means. *More profit.*

Superstars Have a Great Attitude, Aptitude, and Willingness to Learn

It can be tough to find and hire the most skilled players in this market. That means you need to change your hiring approach. Look past a candidate's skills and immediate experience and instead focus on their attitude, aptitude, and willingness to learn.

For example, at A1 Garage Door Service something we look for is the determination to succeed. We know we can teach the skills if the person has a winning attitude. We also look for people who want to help *us* succeed by taking on more responsibility and continuing to learn.

Superstars Are Honest and Ethical

Superstars are honest and ethical. That's another reason to hold out for them. If you hire someone who is dishonest or has compromised ethics and they do something bad while working for you, you risk burning your reputation to the ground and your home service business along with it.

You need to put a system in place to screen employees and stick by it. When you're slammed, you'll be tempted to blow it off. Don't do that, and here's why.

We started a branch of A1 Garage in Michigan with just one employee, our market manager. Soon, we had more business opportunities than one guy could handle, so we were looking to hire another technician.

We didn't have as many qualified applicants as we had hoped for, so we were pretty excited when we found a charismatic, experienced technician who wanted to join our team. We were really slammed at that location and needed him to start immediately, but we had to wait before we could make him an offer. Why? Because at A1 Garage we have a screening process that takes about a week to complete and it starts *before* the person is hired.

We run criminal background checks and require drug screens for all new hires, and every employee who operates a company vehicle has a motor vehicle record check done as well. We do this process because we want to make absolutely sure the person we are sending to our customers' homes is safe and reliable.

Good thing we waited. The background check on this guy revealed information that instantly disqualified him from working for our company.

Given our dire situation, it would have been easy to ignore the red flags and hire him anyway. We chose instead to honor our policy of only hiring ethical and honest people, and we restarted our search.

Sure enough, not too long afterward we found the perfect candidate—qualified, a team player, with a positive attitude and a clean background. As expected, he soon became a superstar employee.

Superstars will pass the background check and you can send them to your customers' homes with confidence. Stick to the program.

Superstars Know Their Worth

When it comes to employees, you get what you pay for. Superstars know their worth. When you're building your team, be willing to pay a little more to get them to come on board. People who are willing to work for cheap often make up for it by mailing it in with substandard work. This lowers morale and leads to higher turnover—all of which will cut into your profit.

If you pay a little more for the best people and treat them well, the profit they create will more than make up for the increased expense.

There is an abundance of amazing employees out there working for average companies who would love the chance to show you what they've got. The key is to find those people and steal them away! The majority of your hires should be amazing people you recruit away from other companies.

At A1 Garage, we have a robust apprentice program where we take energetic, willing, and able people with no experience and build them into great garage door technicians and salespeople.

Superstars Come in a Variety of Personality Types

How do you know what type of person you need in each position? Answer: You sit down with your managers and define it. Have your existing superstars take the DiSC personality profile and look for personality types that match their results. When interviewing, make sure you stay laser focused on finding the exact type of person you want rather than looking for a specific skill set.

When hiring for any of my companies, I hire for determination first, skills second. The importance of a candidate's determination to succeed cannot be overstated. Remember: you can teach people skills, but you can't teach a winning attitude.

Be a Talent Magnet

You should always be recruiting. Major league baseball teams have farm teams that allow them to develop a deep bench of top players they can send to the show when an opening occurs.

That means if you find a superstar, hire them and find a place for them in your company. Having a surplus of good employees on board gives you choices about staffing you wouldn't have otherwise. It also reduces the stress of having to scramble to fill a role with someone you don't know at all.

Speaking of choices, good employees have a lot of them and being recruited brings this fact to the front of their mind. You're asking them to take a risk, so you need to make a strong case for why they should leave their current position and join *your* company.

For example, what makes you special? Is it your friendly, helpful culture? Is your company so awesome people come and stay for years? Do you offer a career rather than just a job? Maybe you have a cool office and always run the latest technology. How about company outings, picnics, employee appreciation days, and awards? On-the-job training, cross-training, and advanced education support and certifications also help, as does a great compensation and benefits package (health insurance, vacation, incentives, bonuses, stock, 401K, etc.).

Make sure all of these reasons why someone should join your organization are written down. Sharing it with employees will make it easier for them to get their superstar colleagues into the pipeline.

Look for Superstars Working in Crappy Jobs

I'm always looking for good people wherever I go. If I'm in a restaurant, gas station, or retail store and I notice someone who has a great work ethic—meaning they are hustling and serving customers with a smile—I will try to get them on my team. I give them my card and say, "If you're looking for a really great career, with paid time off and insurance, call me." I do this at least a couple times a month.

Syndicate Job Postings via Applicant Tracking Systems

We use an applicant tracking system through our payroll service provider. Examples of some applicant tracking systems are Workable and iHire. All we have to do is provide the job description, and the system syndicates it to major employment sites such as Indeed, CareerBuilder, and Monster.

Think of an applicant tracking system like a customer relationship management (CRM) system for employees. It generates the leads, delivers the prospects, and documents the whole hiring process all in one place.

Turn Your Staff into Recruiters

Job ads are good, but the very best way to find superstars is to turn your whole staff into recruiters. To accomplish this task, you'll need to put together an employee referral program that rewards them for bringing in good candidates.

Don't worry; if the employees doing the referrals are good, chances are the people they refer will be too. They won't risk looking bad by recommending people who aren't up to their standards.

A study analyzing 25,000 employees showed several benefits of hiring through referrals—when the person making the referral is the kind of worker you actually want more of! (The converse, naturally, is a bad employee tends to refer more bad employees.) The study said that referred employees create a 25 percent higher profit than those from other hiring sources. As an aspiring home service millionaire, *profit* is exactly what you're after.

Get employees to participate in your referral program by incentivizing them in creative ways. For example, we show our referral rewards just like a physical ad. This makes the reward look a lot more concrete, and it provides that extra push for your employees to take action.

If you're offering cash, turn it into a big mock check and put it in your office. If you're giving out a gift, print stickers of its image and stick them on your employees' desks.

Five Guidelines for a Successful Employee Referral Program:

1. Make it easy and rewarding for your employees to refer their friends and colleagues. We created a website just for this purpose: work4a1.com.
2. Keep your employees informed about who and what the company is looking for.
3. Let employees know how and when the company will contact

the people they referred so they can tell their colleague what's going to happen.

4. Immediately acknowledge each referral and thank the employee for it.

5. Track and measure the results. You want to make sure your employees are referring the right people! If they aren't, you may need to be clearer about your needs.

The superstar employees who have been referred to me, and those I've found and recruited away from my competitors, are the reason I've been able to grow my company to the size it is today.

Advertise on Facebook

Hopefully you already have an attractive and professional-looking Facebook page that you're using to connect with your potential customers.

You'll want to add a jobs tab to your company page and then instruct employees to have their candidates sign up on that page. You can then connect the page to your applicant tracking system.

And since Facebook allows your company to target specific audiences by geography, demographics, and interests, you can also run job ads through Facebook. For example, if you're an HVAC company in Denver looking for techs, you can target candidates within a specific radius of your business with your recruiting message. To increase your reach and generate more traffic to your company page, you'll want to take advantage of Facebook's paid advertising programs.

Important: If you use Facebook for recruiting, make sure you assign someone to watch your company page and follow up with both the applicant (and the referrer, if there is one) as soon as an application comes through.

Landing a Superstar

There are five steps to landing a superstar: prescreening, personality testing, in-person interview, background check, and offer. Here's how we do it at A1 Garage. This process allows you to quickly filter out people who aren't a good fit so you can spend most of your time talking with the cream of the crop.

Prescreening

As you already know, once you have a pool of qualified applicants, you need to screen them thoroughly. Screen all applicants over email and the phone *before* you bring them into the office for an in-person interview.

Email gives you a sense of a candidate's written communication skills, and a phone interview allows you to assess their verbal communication skills. You can quickly determine if their skills match what you need in a certain position and whether they'd be a good fit for your company.

Your goal is to make sure the candidate is perfect for the position so you don't make exceptions. If at any point during the phone conversation you're not sensing a superstar, trust your gut, do both of you a favor, and end the interview.

On the phone, you'll want to ask the usual questions about work experience and skills. Ask questions that help bring out their personality and professional demeanor. These are my top three:

1. Why should I hire you?
2. If I called your old boss, what would he or she tell me you need to work on?
3. How you would handle [insert situation]? (Make it a situational question that requires creative reasoning skills.)

And here are five additional questions you can ask:

1. **What are your career goals? Did you come here for a career or a job?** In a perfect world, the career goals the candidate shares will match your company's needs and they'll talk about those goals with passion and energy.

2. **What are you not interested in doing professionally?** This is another way of asking for weaknesses and it works well.

3. **Who were your last three bosses? When I call them up, how will each of them gauge your performance on a scale of 1 to 10?** What you're doing here is letting them know you're going to call their references. And trust me—it's worth the time to make those phone calls.

   When asked this question, a lot of candidates backpedal and say things like, "We didn't really get along," "I didn't appreciate their chain of command," "The dispatcher was a jerk," or "The appointment setter screwed me." When they make comments like that, you know the person won't be a good hire.

   The other thing you can do to see if the person is a good fit for your culture is check them out on Yelp. To do this, go to Yelp and click on "Find Friends" and enter their email address. You want to see a lot of five-star reviews. It's OK if they have a few one-star reviews; you just don't want the profile to be filled with them. Then, check out their social media profiles. Who are they are hanging out with? Do they look and sound like a fit with your company culture? Make sure the things they are posting are aligned with the values of your company.

4. **What were some low points during your last job?** Maybe there was an installation that went wrong and the customer was unhappy. Also ask them if they would change anything about their last job and, if so, what the top three things would be. This will tell you a lot about their personality type. What you want to hear is that they take responsibility even though it might not be their fault and they have an improvement plan to proactively fix things.

5. **What kind of money do you need to make to survive?** While you can't ask too many personal questions—you absolutely *cannot* ask if they're married, for example—one thing I've learned is to make sure the possible candidates have a decent standard of living. What I've noticed over time is that if a guy only needs $400 a week to survive, he or she will work hard Monday and Tuesday until they make what they need and then fall back for the rest of the week. But when they've got bills to pay, they tend to be motivated to earn more money, especially if they are paid based on commission.

Personality Testing

The purpose of personality testing is to make sure the candidate has the type of personality you know can excel in that position.

The DiSC personality profile is a really useful tool. It allows you to get a sense of who the person is and how they think, which can help you determine how likely it is that they'll be a good fit for the job you're looking to fill.

You can ask job applicants to complete a DiSC test (at your expense, not theirs) and have them forward you the test report. Visit homeservicemillionaire.com/personality-test for more information.

In-Person Interview

The interview—or series of interviews—is where you and your team have the first opportunity to interact face-to-face with the applicant. Every applicant is an actor auditioning for a part and most will tell you what they think you want to hear. They may even agree with everything you say and seem like the "perfect" candidate. *Don't be fooled!* Your job is to get behind the mask that every candidate wears.

Remember, you want a superstar. You're looking for the person who becomes *more* effective in the face of adversity. So push back! A superstar may start to question your reasoning—or even tell you that you're wrong. The ideal candidate will try to qualify you just as they would a prospective client! Here are five things you can do to stack the deck in your favor when it comes to interviewing:

Establish a Relaxed Atmosphere: Stiffness and formality favors the applicant. Your goal is to make them feel relaxed so they drop their guard. Interview them through free-flowing conversation rather than conducting a structured Q&A. The first step is to establish a rapport with the candidate. Break the ice by asking them about an experience listed on their resume. To test for cultural fit, ask open-ended questions such as, "What would we need to do as a company to encourage you to go the extra mile, push harder, and do whatever it takes to exceed expectations?" Remember, the goal is to have a two-way conversation, not just a back-and-forth where the candidate is answering a bunch of canned questions with rehearsed responses.

Dig Deep: Remind the candidate that hiring decisions at your company are made based on personality profile rather than purely on skill set, and ask them if they agree having the right personality for the job is more important. They'll likely say yes. Once they do, tell them you'd like to find out what shaped them as an employee. Start with their earliest work experiences. Ask, "What were some of the biggest challenges in your life? They don't need to be work related." Uncover their areas of accomplishment. Try to determine if they're an overachiever in any area. Ask them to tell you about a time in their life when the odds were stacked against them, yet they overcame them and succeeded. (By the way, this is Elon Musk's favorite interview question.) Ask if they have ever practiced and reached a high level in any area of life. You are looking for someone who wants to go beyond just getting by in life.

Ask the candidate to rate themselves on a scale of 1 to 10 in various areas, such as ambition, confidence, ability to create desire in others, time management, and presentation skills. Beware of any candidate who claims to be a "10" in every area. They may be that good, but it's more likely they are just plain narcissistic.

Gauge their empathy and ability to bond with others by asking them to tell you about a time they helped a coworker even though it wasn't required.

Ask how dedicated they are to self-improvement. What was the last self-help book they read? Are they taking any courses or seminars, or getting professional certifications? You're looking for someone with a growth mindset (believes they can always be getting better) rather than a fixed mindset (believes they're as good now as they'll ever be). You want to hire people who can and will grow at the same speed as your company.

Make Them Sell You on Hiring Them: Make the candidate sell you on hiring them for the position. Say, "Thank you, this sounds good, but I'm not getting the impression that you're a superstar." They have to really believe you think they don't have what it takes to succeed in your business.

Tell the candidate about a business problem or opportunity you face, real or hypothetical, and ask what they'd do. Ask them to explain *why* they decided on the approach they chose. Superstars will never give up because they have faith in themselves.

When in doubt, *don't hire.* If you're not sure about a candidate, take more time. Keep looking. Take the long-range view and do not hire until you've found the right person. (The cost of a bad hire is crazy high.)

As the saying goes, "Hire slow, fire fast." This means don't hire someone until you are positive they're going to excel.

Once in a while, even after all that due diligence, you'll realize a new hire doesn't fit. If that happens, do not wait. Fire them quickly.

Superstars are worth the wait. The more you challenge them, the more you encourage them to overachieve. But remember to reward them when they meet and exceed your challenges and expectations!

Put Them "On the Job": Once you've narrowed your list to the final three candidates, sit down with them and go through some scenarios they would face on the job. Show them a list of all the expectations for the job and make sure they read and agree with them.

At this point, I like to send the candidate out with at least two of their future coworkers for ride-alongs. I then ask my guys exactly how things went and what they think of the candidate. I do the same thing with dispatchers and call center reps.

Do you test-drive a new car before buying it? You probably do. So why don't you do the same when it comes to hiring someone new? I've had people ace the interview only to discover that once mixed in with existing employees they weren't a fit with our company culture.

Background Check

If they've made it this far, it's time for the background check. Do it. Every time. No exceptions. What you don't know *can* hurt you.

Offer

They've passed all the tests. Now it's time to make the offer. Work with your financial or HR person to understand what the compensation for each role on the organizational chart should be. Don't be cheap. You want A players, and A players know their worth.

Let the candidate know there will be a nondisclosure agreement (NDA) and a noncompete agreement. Tell them there is a 90-day trial period with continued employment conditional on successful training. Don't put new employees in a truck by themselves until they are trained and have proven themselves.

I once let somebody make it through training that I knew would not last. Big mistake! It ended up costing me a lot of money and my company's reputation took a hit. If they're failing during training, do both of you a favor and let them go.

Other Ways to Hire

There are also other ways to hire people, such as internships and on contract.

Interns

I *love* paid interns and have hired many into full-time positions at my company. There's no introductory period because I already know their strengths and weaknesses. I know their performance and if they're truly cut out for the gig. If the intern gets along with every coworker and their direct supervisor is advocating for them, he or she probably deserves an offer of a full-time position.

Contractors

I'm also getting more into hiring contract people for some of the administrative roles in my company (e.g., accounting, tax preparation, payroll, marketing, lead generation, and IT) because it allows me to more easily calibrate the talent I need in those positions as my company grows.

Family

Finally, a word about hiring family members. If you're lucky, they'll have the right attitude and skills. If not, you're in for some drama because it's very hard to be impartial when it comes to the hard decisions we're required to make as owners. It's so easy for everyone involved to end up hating each other. Very rarely do I see family and friends together in a business working out 100 percent. People will try to make it work until somebody cracks.

That said, I grew up working in my family's business in Michigan and was very fortunate that my mom, dad, and stepdad all got along and formed an amazing team. What made it work was huge, mutual respect. But I know now that is really unusual.

When hiring family, proceed with caution.

In the home service industry, our business is all about people. Finding the people who are able to get things done and are a match with your company culture is what will allow your business to thrive and attract even more top performers.

Performance- or Commission-Based Pay

Should home service techs be paid only a straight salary or hourly rate, or should they also be paid on commission?

The most common argument in favor of a straight paycheck is that it removes the temptation to needlessly upsell the customer and keeps the employee from rushing to one job from another just to collect higher commissions.

OK. But you hired superstars, and superstars love an incentive-based pay scale, typically a commission that's based on a percentage of sales revenue they bring in. It also could be a bonus based on a specific performance metric.

Performance-based pay also encourages slowing down and doing the job right the first time. Callbacks can go down, because no one wants to do twice the work for the same pay.

Incentive plans give staffers something to aim for, which leads to increased levels of productivity.

Rewarding superstars for their high performance fosters loyalty. This is especially true if incentive plans have residual value. For example, if the tech gets a bonus for selling a service agreement, they also get a residual bonus for every subsequent year that customer renews.

Performance- and commission-based pay provides motivation for people to get better at their jobs. They'll work harder to increase their knowledge and become better communicators, resulting in more money for them and more profit for you.

Note: There are a million different approaches to incentive plans, so make sure you and your financial or HR person take the time to thoroughly analyze the advantages and disadvantages of each before you select and implement one.

Managing Your Superstars

Having hired the best people for your home service company, now you need to *manage* them. The job of a manager is to help employees stay productive and foster their loyalty. It's also their job to make sure employees have the tools and training necessary to meet and exceed the standards set for them.

Every organization needs managers, and I'm not talking about dictators. Research shows the most effective managers are like coaches who are responsible for creating a team and getting the very best from each team member. Charles Schwab once said, "I consider my ability to arouse enthusiasm among men the greatest asset I possess. The way to develop the best that is in a man is by appreciation and encouragement." The best way to get the best from people is to train them on your way of doing things.

Training Is Essential

All employees need to be formally trained on your policies and procedures. This is nonnegotiable. Otherwise, there's no way to be sure they know what they are doing or that everyone is doing things the same way—your way. Structured training programs also allow you to get a lot of new hires up to speed—fast. And in the home service business, the more techs you have to send out, the more opportunities there are to make money!

So, how fast could you train 20 new employees right now?

I rest my case.

You can outsource the training or do it all in-house. The important thing is that there is a process everyone follows and that it happens. Continuous training is critical to your ability to grow and scale your business. Your job is to make sure:

1. Employees know and understand what is considered good performance and attitude.
2. Employees are brought up to speed on technology as it is introduced.
3. Skill levels are consistent throughout the company. When they are, job and project results are predictable and variations are easily detected. Record your inbound calls by using a service such as Callcap. It's legal in most states as long as you announce the call is being recorded for training and quality purposes. Then, have the customer service representatives (CSRs) listen to their calls. Most have no idea what they sound like! For more information, visit homeservicemillionaire.com/call-tracking.

4. Every employee has a manual outlining your policies and procedures relevant to their job.

5. The procedures outlined in those manuals are so ingrained in the culture that when asked certain questions or presented with problems, every employee offers the same response.

6. All managers are working off the same playbook. If an employee asks a question or has a problem, all managers should offer a similar answer.

7. Customers are all treated the same way across the company, no matter whom they deal with.

8. There is a robust online library of information, such as how-to videos and documentation, which employees can access to get better at their jobs.

The Morning Mojo Call

For 20 minutes every morning, we have a team meet in the conference room. Remote employees join us on our conference line. It's called our morning mojo call. It allows us to get on the same page, do some role-plays, celebrate wins, and reinforce our values. It's a great way to start the day. Here's what's on the agenda:

1. **Accountability:** Everybody gets to see what the guys' average tickets are.

2. **Updates:** Managers give updates on the CRM system and technology, go over sales, and so on.

3. **Role-playing:** During this section, I pull somebody to the front of the room and we go over different selling strategies. This involves role-playing, and it's the most effective tool in our sales playbook. One role-play game we love at these meetings is to see who can always answer a question with another question.

It goes something like this:

> **Me (pretending to be a client):** "Tell me all about your company!"
>
> **Employee:** "Absolutely, what exactly would you like to know about us?" Or, "Before I dive into that, have you had any past experience with our business?"

Teaching people how to answer a question with a question will give them a lot of insights about what customers really want and put them in a position to earn the sale.

After each role-play, we give each other feedback on how to do things faster and sell more products.

4. **Celebration:** We review and celebrate the five-star Yelp reviews and the happy customer letters we've received.
5. **Values:** We also take time to reinforce the importance of ethics and honesty in everything we do.

Expecting and Inspecting

A while back I hired a fantastic manager who came from a white-collar industry. We got along pretty well, but we had a huge disagreement about one of my favorite taglines: "People do what you inspect, not what you expect."

His perspective was, "If you trust your employees to do the right thing, you have no idea how great they can become."

Now, after three years of working with us, his attitude sounds more like this: "Inspect the living shit out of them."

People do what you inspect, not what you expect. Make sure you have a process in place to check and see if people are really doing their jobs the way you want them to be done.

Mentoring a New Manager

Managers need training and mentoring too, and sometimes the best way to do it is to take them along with you. Here's an example of how I did just that with a new manager.

At 10:00 p.m. one night my mobile phone rang. It was Joe, a new manager who had just started with us.

He said, "Hey, Tommy. There's an emergency repair job at a residence about 40 minutes away from me, but I can't get in a truck—I'm already two beers deep over here."

I said, "No problem. I'll cover it. What's the address and phone number?"

Joe gave me the information and then said, "Hey, can I go with you? I'd like to see how you approach this type of job."

I said, "Sure!"

I picked him up and on the way over to the job he started asking me questions. I said, "Joe, the most important thing to do on the way to a customer's house is call them. This gives you a chance to feel them out and understand what kind of situation you are walking into!"

I admit I was on a mission that evening because this was the first job I had run with this particular manager. I wanted to show him how it is done!

I dialed the customer's number and a man picked up. He immediately began asking me a lot of questions about things I wouldn't know until I got there and diagnosed the job. It was also hard to understand what he was saying because he didn't speak English very well.

I hung up with the guy and said to Joe, "Did you hear that? Sounds to me like this guy is going to need to be convinced we know what we are doing and are honest."

We got to the job and greeted the customer, who followed us into the garage to watch what we were doing. Upon inspection of the garage panel, I noticed a small crack. I also determined the garage door opener was not working properly because of a problem with the gear and sprocket.

We started with the opener. The customer wanted to validate our findings, so I had him climb up the ladder so he could see the problems with the gear and sprocket himself. As the customer observed our repair process, we explained what we were doing every step of the way.

Once I was finished repairing the gear and sprocket, I told the customer about the crack in the garage panel and said it was what had caused the damage to the gear. Again, I got the customer up on the ladder and let him find the crack. He came down and asked me how we could fix it. I told him, "With a strut." Then he got back on the ladder and said, "Tom, oh no, I found another one!"

I told the customer, "Great job!" and informed him we would need to add another strut, and he was all for it!

When we had finished installing the two struts, I told him to lift the door up. It should have been light enough to lift manually with one hand. He tried to lift it and said, "Oh no, so heavy." Then he asked what the long-term solution was. I said we'd need to replace the torsion springs.

Once the springs were in place, the customer went to lift the door with one hand and it went up as smooth as butter!

The garage door has been working since then with no complaints and will continue to work for a very long time.

We delivered maximum value, not only by showing up late at night but also by fixing the door the right way the first time.

We made that customer happy, but more importantly, my new manager got to see me practice what I preach. I showed Joe how to max out a ticket ethically simply by listening to the customer and observing the job environment, and then giving the customer the opportunity to optimize the performance of his garage door. We covered sales, customer service, and customer relations all in one shot!

Create a Place for Top Talent

Talent comes in a lot of different packages. Sometimes you'll meet someone who isn't quite a fit for an existing role, but whose skills, if applied properly, could make you money. In that case, see if you can create a role for the person that will allow you to leverage that talent.

For example, we once interviewed a guy with a ton of experience who talked a big game. That raised a few flags, but he passed the background check and we decided to send him to our Prescott, Arizona, office to test him out as a technician.

He was a fine tech, but when it came to sales, he was a *beast*. In fact, he had the highest sales ticket of any tech I'd ever had!

The problem was he was totally inconsistent about showing up on time to customers, communicating with the office, and accurately completing the administrative tasks that were part of his job and critical to the success of my business!

Since a business is ownership and control of a system, this inability to work within our system did not work for my managers or me, and we soon had to part ways.

A month later, this tech called me begging for his job back, but none of my managers would get on board with it. On one hand, I understood my managers' position, but on the other hand, I kept thinking about those huge ticket sales. I had to find a way to maximize that incredible sales talent without upsetting people and compromising my own CRM system. So I decided to create a training company within my company group, and hired him as a trainer on contract.

He is now traveling for me, going to markets all over the country to train technicians on how to be better at sales, installs, and customer service. By structuring his pay on performance and having others hold him accountable, I created a role for him that suited his personality and skills. He continues to be a huge asset to the company.

Speaking of sales, great salespeople can make a huge difference in your company. Look for people who are self-motivated and used to working hard. Some of A1 Garage's best employees grew up on farms or are former college athletes! And remember to get them to sign an NDA. Visit homeservicemillionaire.com/resources for a template.

Retaining Superstar Employees

Stephen Covey once said, "Always treat your employees exactly as you want them to treat your best customers." Superstars are always in demand, so you can pretty much assume they're being asked weekly to take a job with your competitor. Make it hard for them to think about moving by providing them with a career path, paying them fairly, and making sure they feel appreciated for their contributions to your company. Retaining key employees is a lot cheaper than recruiting new ones. Do whatever you can to keep them on board.

Money is important, but you also want to make sure there are reasons to stay outside of money. A good work culture—including company events such as potluck dinners and barbeques—is good, and flexible hours also go a long way to make people want to stay, especially people reentering the workforce or parents who have kids at home.

Dealing with Negative Employees

Despite your best efforts, sometimes you make a bad hire and you find yourself with a problem employee. Or maybe you buy a business and inherit an employee with attitude issues. Over time, a negative person will drag down your entire team. You'll find them gossiping by the water cooler, the loading dock, the kitchen, and other hard-to-police places, spreading their message of doom and gloom. If they're within the 90-day test period, and you have the necessary documentation, fire them. But if they've been there for a while or you've inherited them from a company you've acquired, it may not be that easy. Then what?

Optimally, there should be an operating manual in place that outlines your expectations in terms of job performance and behaviors. If you are still in the process of putting an operating manual into place (and I hope you are), here is a way you can deal with it in the interim.

First and foremost, document, document, document. Not just the behaviors, but also the negative effect they are having on the business. Include descriptions of specific verbal and physical behaviors and actions that concern you, damage productivity, hurt team morale, or reflect badly on the organization. Remember to record nonverbal behaviors such as rolling eyes, sulking, avoiding work, and wasting time on social media.

Next, sit down privately with the employee to discuss his or her attitude problem. Try to determine if there is a reason for their behavior. Describe the behaviors you will no longer tolerate and tell the employee what behavior you expect instead, such as cooperation, helpfulness, and courteousness. Tell them if they fix the problem, all will be forgiven, but if it persists the next step will be a written warning.

If they continue with the behavior, write them up and explain that the next step is a three-day suspension. If they are still not on board after that, it's time to provide them with an opportunity to work for your competitor.

Remember that complaint forms, personnel files, performance reviews, and discipline warnings must comply with applicable labor laws. If in doubt, consult your organization's attorney or HR expert.

The other kind of employee negativity you may run into is when employees become unhappy because they believe something bad about your organization. This can happen for a number of reasons. Maybe you made a decision that was in the best interest of the company but it adversely affected the staff. Maybe you were in a hurry and glossed over someone's legitimate question in a staff meeting. Or maybe employees are feeling insecure because they heard a rumor you were losing a big customer and were going to have to lay people off.

Whatever the cause of the workplace discontent, as the leader you must address the issue. If you don't, unhappiness will fester beneath the surface and, like a volcano, it'll eventually erupt and cause even more damage.

The best way to combat workplace negativity is to keep it from occurring in the first place. Make a positive, helpful, and healthy attitude part of the mission, vision, and values of your company. Hire people who light up the room when they walk in and bend over backward to help others around them.

Above all, be honest with your staff. A lack of open communication leads to distrust, dissatisfaction, cynicism, and turnover. In times of uncertainty, you and your managers should engage openly with your staff, facilitating communication and encouraging feedback.

Take a Hard Line against Theft

I once had a technician who not only stole merchandise, but also installed an opener, took the customer's check, and wrote his own name on it!

When this happened I immediately filed a police report, and now he will be going to jail for a long time for fraud and theft. I know of one owner who had a technician arrested during the middle of a meeting after he had stolen from his company!

We've talked about how important it is to do a thorough background check on potential hires (including a drug test). But if someone slips through the cracks, you have to act fast.

But why file a police report and have a thief arrested? Because you need everyone to know what the consequences are if you catch them stealing from you. They need to know you will act swiftly and you won't back down.

Keep a police report on hand and show it to the candidate when discussing ethics and honesty during the interview. Voilà, no theft.

Develop checks and balances to detect possible cases of theft early and deter them from happening. For example, I use a company called Verizon Networkfleet to keep track of our trucks and let me know when they need to be serviced. Also, if somebody is on a job for more than 20 minutes and does not collect $100 or more, that's a red flag. You can stay on top of this by having your dispatch center call each job to see how it went. Learn more at homeservicemillionaire.com/truck-tracking.

You Are Responsible

For their service in the 2006 Battle of Ramadi, Navy SEAL Team Three's Task Unit Bruiser and its commander Jocko Willink became the most highly decorated special operations unit of the Iraq War. In a *Forbes* interview, Jocko revealed what he thought was the single most important aspect of leadership: the willingness to take responsibility when things go badly. "Leadership starts with ownership—ownership of everything," he said.

Problems with employees come with the territory, but the one thing you do have control over is making sure you take ownership of everything that happens in your business, good and bad.

What does this mean for the owner of a home service company? It means if one of your employees screws up on a job and you've got an angry customer, you don't blame the employee for the problem. The reality is *you're* the boss. *You* hired this employee. *You* trained this employee. *You* pay this employee to represent your company. Therefore, if something goes wrong, you'd better step up and take a hard look at why it happened and figure out how to fix it. Take ownership. You are responsible. ▶▶▶

CHAPTER 7

TIME TO GET GOING

Man, it is so hard to let this book go to print because even as I write this there are so many new things I've learned that I wish I could share here. But as my editor pointed out, if I don't stop now, this book is never going to get done and it won't be able to help anyone!

I hope you picked up some insights, strategies, and tactics you can use to move your home service business forward. To benefit from it, however, you have to carve out the time to do something with this information.

Don't wait. Pick something from this book and put it into practice right away, even if it's just making a list of things you need to do. Then start ticking things off that list. Eventually you will build momentum and your business will start to change. Block out time on your calendar, even if it's just an hour a week, to do something to move your business forward.

You might be thinking, "Reading books like this is doing something," and you're right. (And thank you for reading this one!) The problem is, if all you ever do is read about the things you could (and should) be doing, and never actually do any of them, nothing in your business is going to change. I don't want that to happen to you.

If you have a hard time getting started or staying in motion, you may need to reach out to someone who will hold you accountable to do what you need to do to get to where you say you want to go. Pick someone whose opinion you value, who you wouldn't want to disappoint, and who isn't afraid to dish out a little tough love if you keep coming to the table with nothing done.

Know that you're going to make mistakes. Don't worry about that. I make lots of mistakes. Anyone who is out there making stuff happen day after day is making mistakes. The difference is we don't dwell on them. You don't have time to beat yourself up over every mistake. Develop the mental discipline to make a quick note of what happened and figure out where you need to adjust. Then forget about it and move on to the next thing. Take care of the problems, but focus most of your attention and energy on what you can control and make happen.

Also keep in mind that no matter how good you are, life is going to throw you a curveball once in a while. Bad stuff will happen. Don't let it throw you too much and don't give up. Just learn from it. And keep going. That's what I do, and it has allowed me to build a multi-million-dollar business with more than 250 employees in 12 states. And that kind of persistence is what will allow you to do the same thing.

Do whatever it takes to make your business a place where you love going in no matter what day it is. If there is an employee you dread seeing, get a different employee! If the office or warehouse is a mess, clean it up.

Finally, search out and hire people who are better than you at everything possible and delegate responsibility for everything that makes sense. It's the only way you'll be able to get your life back and have time to do everything you need to do to ensure your destiny as a home service millionaire.

I've had a blast putting this book together for you, and I'm looking forward to hearing about how it has helped you. Email me with your comments and feedback at tommy@homeservicemillionaire.com. I look forward to hearing about your home service millionaire milestones. ▶▶▶

ACKNOWLEDGMENTS

I want to thank the army of people who came together to make this book a reality so it can help you in your quest to become a home service millionaire.

First, I want to thank my family—especially my dad Tom Sr., my mom Gina, and my stepdad Bill—without whose influence and support I wouldn't be where I am today.

Thanks also to my beautiful sister, Kia, who makes me an expert at arguing, keeps me on my toes, and gives me more love than I could ever hope to give back. Thank you for being you and having the most amazing family a little brother could ever ask for.

To my best friend and amazing person, Gabe, who was the catalyst for this crazy garage door service business journey, thanks buddy for your steady friendship and constant inspiration.

To the amazing contributors in this book—Mike Davis, Jaime DiDomenico, Brian Kaskavalciyan, Erica Leonor, Marc Levesque, Al Levi, Darius Lyvers, Ara Mahdessian, Darryl Margaux and Matt Glickman, Ellen Rohr, Fred Silberstein and Brian Cohen, and Craig Smith—thank you so much for your time and generosity. I know what you shared will make a big difference for everyone who reads it.

Thank you to Hillary, my awesome friend, who encourages me to be the best person I can be every day. From you I've learned to be considerate of others, to smile when things aren't going my way, and to never, ever give up. I am a far better man for having you in my life.

A shout-out to my general manager Adam Cronenberg, my market development master Rob Hennard, and my business partner

Dustin Armstrong, whose hard word and dedication have been massively instrumental to the success of A1 Garage Door Service and more. Big props also go to Shannon Neal, the backbone of the A1 marketing team and a great friend. A1 wouldn't be in growth mode without him.

Thanks to Gianni Cara and his marketing team for working tirelessly to get the word out to you about all of my business efforts, especially the Home Service Expert.

I also want to thank my editor, Helena Bouchez of Executive Words, for bringing this book together—a book I hope changes your life the way the information in it has changed mine.

I realize there are many, many more of you who have contributed to my success, but to mention you all by name I would have to double the size of this book. Know that I noticed and appreciated all the efforts that allowed me to make this book a reality.

Finally, to my amazing teams at A1 Garage Door Service and other business entities: there's no way I could have made it to where I am without you. You show me every day that we're stronger paddling together. (To see the A1 Garage team, visit homeservicemillionaire.com/A1.) ▶▶▶

RESOURCES

Here are the top five ways to get more information on how to grow your home service business into the millions:

1. Check out a full list of resources, including all the links I referenced in this book, at **homeservicemillionaire.com/resources**.

2. Subscribe to the Home Service Expert podcast at **homeserviceexpert.com/podcast**.

3. Register for our webinar to learn how we can help you grow your business at **homeserviceexpert.com/webinar**.

4. Register for the Home Service Millionaire Book Club at **homeservicemillionaire.com/book-club**. To get started, here are 14 books every home service business owner should read:

   2 Second Lean by Paul A. Akers
   How to Win Friends and Influence People by Dale Carnegie
   Influence: Science and Practice by Robert B. Cialdini
   The Richest Man in Babylon by George S. Clason
   The E-Myth Revisited by Michael E. Gerber
   The Ultimate Sales Machine by Chet Holmes
   Rich Dad Poor Dad by Robert T. Kiyosaki
   The 7-Power Contractor by Al Levi
   Buyology by Martin Lindstrom

Bluefishing by Steve Sims
Start with Why by Simon Sinek
The Millionaire Next Door by Thomas J. Stanley and
     William D. Danko
The Automatic Customer by John Warrillow
Traction by Gino Wickman

5. If you *really* want to jump-start your home service business, book a free discovery call with a Home Service Expert coach at **homeserviceexpert.com/discovery-call.**

BONUS: SELLING YOUR BUSINESS

Everything in this book is designed to help you build a robust and profitable business that will pay you handsomely as long as you care to run it. At some point, however, you may decide you want to retire to a tropical paradise or just move on to other things.

That's why I want to make sure you know how to get the best deal possible when selling your business. I've tapped my colleagues Fred Silberstein and Brian Cohen at SF&P Advisors, experts in buying and selling home service companies, to tell you exactly what's involved in selling a business and what you need to do to prepare. Here are the 10 steps you need to take to get ready for this big transition.

PREPARING TO SELL

Fred Silberstein and Brian Cohen, SF&P Advisors

1. Get your financials in order: You want accurate income statements that are prepared in accordance with generally accepted accounting principles (GAAP). To be safe, have your accountant prepare these statements or at least review them for compliance. This should be done well in advance of selling because you want to be able to show consistency when prior periods are compared to your competitors.

2. Build your service contract base: Buyers love the fence that a service contract puts around the customer base. (Now you know how!)

3. Have an appropriate marketing plan: There is a difference between the various stages of a business (i.e., growth vs. maturity). As you are growing your business, your marketing spend should be higher. There is spending to build a brand vs. spending to capitalize on an existing large customer base.

4. Consider acquisitions: The more revenue, the higher the price. If you can eliminate back office or take advantage of buying power, you will see that one plus one can equal more than two.

5. Build out your management team: Presenting a management team with a solid bench is significant for a buyer. Buyers want to see that the business is not only reliant on the person selling it.

6. Make the decision to sell (and don't waffle): Selling a business is what we do every day. For you, the seller, this is very emotional. The business may have been built across generations or represent a significant personal contribution on your part over a period of many years.

7. Discuss valuations and expectations: Get very clear on all of your deal objectives, including price, terms, future employment, earn-outs, etc. We see people change the goals of a transaction midstream all the time. Communication with your advisors is key. We recommend you have regularly scheduled calls with your advisors to discuss the transaction.

8. Hire an intermediary: This may sound self-serving on our part, but think about it: you are going to need to focus your attention on continuing to run the business in "ordinary course," meaning run it in a way where revenue or service doesn't fall off, which could jeopardize the deal. Having an intermediary allows your interests to be represented without you having to participate directly with a buyer. This becomes even more important if you have an ongoing relationship with the buyer. Plus, a certain level of knowledge comes with doing transactions every day. The intermediary should also control the document flow and marketing materials, such as teasers and confidential information memoranda.

9: Understand the diligence process: When a buyer is looking to acquire your business, they are going to do a deep dig into all things financial, operational, legal, and tax. Having a person on the inside to handle those requests is key because the process generally takes 90 days or more.

10. Choose an attorney who specializes in transactions: You need someone who is proficient in the various legal aspects of selling a company. A generalist usually won't be fluent or have the knowledge or experience required to act so things go smoothly.

For more information on how to sell your home service business, visit homeservicemillionaire.com/sell-your-home-service-business.

ABOUT THE AUTHOR

Tommy Mello is the owner and operator of A1 Garage Door Service; the host of the Home Service Expert podcast; and the owner, partner, or investor in 14 other businesses ranging from Christmas lights to real estate to mobile apps.

In 2010, Tommy became the sole owner and operator of a single Phoenix-based garage door service business, which came with $50,000 in debt. Today, A1 Garage generates more than $30 million dollars in annual revenue, with more than 250 employees in 12 states, and its ambition is to reach a billion dollars in sales within the next five years.

A voracious learner who reads at least one book a week, Tommy is also a master connector who has forged mutually beneficial relationships with dozens of experts in the home service industry. Believing "a rising tide lifts all boats," Tommy immediately shares what he learns with other home service business owners through his podcast, blog, articles, and this book.

Tommy is a regular contributor to *Inc.*, *Entrepreneur*, and other business publications on the topic of entrepreneurship and small business as well as a sought-after podcast, radio, and television guest. When not in the office or working on the businesses, you'll find him on a plane headed to exotic destinations or chasing the little white ball around one of Arizona's many golf courses.

Made in United States
Troutdale, OR
10/11/2023

13596776R00106